ɔUɔ.

SAVE
OUR
SISTERS

An action guide for
helping girls and women
at risk worldwide

Deborah
Meroff

PILOT BOOKS

SOS: Save Our Sisters
by Deborah Meroff

© 2014 Deborah Meroff

Published in the USA by

PILOT BOOKS
Hull, GA. 30646, USA

Email - customerservice@rollinspilot.com

All Scripture quotations, unless otherwise indicated, are taken from THE HOLY BIBLE, NEW INTERNATIONAL VERSION®, NIV® Copyright © 1973, 1978, 1984, 2011 by Biblica, Inc.™ Used by permission. All rights reserved worldwide.

ISBN 9780981869698

Printed in the United States of America

Contents

Foreword

It is a great privilege to write a Foreword for this action guide, which is an abbreviated version of *True Grit: Women Taking on the World, for God's Sake*—one of the most important books in my life, especially in the last 10 years. It's been a joy to give away as well as sell tens of thousands of copies all over the world, in five different languages besides English. It was my book of the year when it first came out, and then book of the decade. OM International's "Special Projects" funded many of the translations and we are thrilled to have this useful new version.

You might find it hard to read too much of this at a time. The realities of what girls and women have suffered and continue to suffer represent some of the most serious human rights violations in our world today. But these pages also encourage us to see what God can do through us.

It is my prayer that you will not only read this timely and important guide, but that you will get involved in distributing it. We are all people commissioned for ministry and we can increase our impact when we give away great books like this. God bless you as you do your part.

Dr. George Verwer
Founder and International Director Emeritus
OM International

Introduction

A decade ago, compelled by a dozen years of observations as an international journalist, I wrote the first edition of *TRUE GRIT: Women Taking on the World for God's Sake.* I hoped that by the time this revised and updated *SOS* guide was published I could report sweeping advances in the status quo of girls and women worldwide. However, while some excellent human rights measures are being passed in many countries, efforts to enforce these new laws have been far from adequate. The tragic reality is that violence, trafficking and gender discrimination on many fronts is actually on the increase for millions of females living in the 21st Century.

SOS: SAVE OUR SISTERS is intentionally subtitled. *An Action Guide for Helping Women and Girls At Risk Worldwide.* This book does without the stories of international women included in *TRUE GRIT*; it is a streamlined, A to Z reference to the human rights issues most effecting half our world's population. While this overview is not by any means comprehensive; it should serve as a useful guide and stimulus for further investigation.

My purpose in writing this *SOS*, however, is not just to inform. It is my fervent hope that the disturbing facts will spur readers into action. For many people the most obvious and powerful first response will be intercession, but groups and individuals are also urged to take the suggested "Action Steps." Every voice, every letter of protest and every penny of support is critical if we are to join in solidarity against these widespread abuses, and effect change.

Be warned. Passionate prayers not only change the world, they have a way of transforming the people who pray them. As God channels His concern through you, you may find yourself responding in unexpected ways. I hope so. It's time for us all to adopt the resolution so well expressed by activist and clergyman Edward Everett Hale:

"I am only one; but still I am one. I cannot do everything; but I can do something.... And what I should do, by the grace of God, I will do."

Deborah Meroff
http://Women-Without-Borders.net

SOS: Brides at Risk

Every year up to 25,000 brides are deliberately set on fire in India, Pakistan, Bangladesh and Nepal. In India alone, a dowry-related death takes place almost every hour.[1] Most of these murders go unpunished.

BRIDE BURNING

India and Nepal: Although the payment of a dowry has been legally banned in India for over 50 years and more recently in other parts of the subcontinent, marriage gifts from the bride's family are usually still considered indispensible. Since a wife is often looked upon as a liability, she is expected to pay her way. This means coming up with exorbitant amounts of money or valuables (averaging the equivalent of five times the family's annual income). It is therefore unsurprising when destitute families dread the birth of a girl. In fact, the dowry system is a direct cause for the escalating numbers of girl babies being killed. (See "Vital Statistics: Female Infanticide and Feticide"). Some teenage girls, knowing their fathers are unable to pay a bride price, have been known to commit suicide.

A woman's status in her husband's house is determined by the dowry she brings with her. Sparks may fly if the groom's family decides the previously agreed-upon dowry isn't enough. They may try extortion, and if her family cannot meet their demands, the bride is in danger of abuse, divorce and even death so that the groom can marry again for another dowry.

Battered wives have few options. Very rarely will their families take them back because of the social stigma of harboring a married daughter. The government provides few shelters for abused women. Most that do exist have such an appalling reputation for their treatment of vulnerable women that they would rather suffer the blows of their husband or in-laws.

Ironically, death rates have increased as India becomes more prosperous. Officially recorded fatalities have shot up from 1,912 in 1987 to 8,391 in 2010, meaning a bride was burned every 90 minutes, according to statistics released by India's National Crime Records Bureau. In most cases the bride's husband or in-laws poured kerosene oil over her and set her afire, hoping the incident would pass for a suicide or an accident with the kitchen stove. Other women have been burned with acid. Those who survive are scarred for life, physically, mentally and emotionally. But the statistics show only the official figures. Thousands of deaths go unreported, and a relatively small number of murderers are punished.

Bangladesh: The dowry system contradicts both religion and law in this Muslim-majority country. Originally the groom's family made a payment to the bride's parents: However, dowry payments from the bride's family have become so much in demand among both rich and poor (in spite of a Dowry Prohibition Act in 1980) that many poor families are unable to get their daughters married. A Domestic Violence Act was passed in 2010 which does not seem to have made much difference, either. Police records showed dowry-related violence hit 7,079 cases in 2011 and 4,563 in the first nine months of 2012.[2].

Pakistan: Bride-burning has also caught on in Pakistan. According to the country's Progressive Women's Association, burning accounts for the violent death of at least 300 women each year, most often at the hands of their husbands or husbands' families. Again, police are usually told the victim was killed by an exploding stove, and there is no prosecution. While divorce is possible in Pakistan, some families decide to rid themselves of unwanted wives by murdering them.

"BRIDES OF THE QUR'AN"

Her wedding day has arrived. Friends and relatives of the young bride-to-be prepare her for the ceremony, bathing and carefully dressing her in finest silk and jewels. Several hours more are devoted to the artful arrangement of her hair and application of makeup. Finally the bride is led forth. She places her hand on the holy book of Islam and repeats her vows. She is now a married woman.

Except that she has no husband.

Her parents have just followed a very old and not uncommon tradition accepted in the rural areas of Pakistan by prominent (Syed) Sindh families, and in some parts of the Punjab.[3] Daughters may only marry within the family—often first cousins—in order to keep the family line pure and its wealth intact. So if suitable candidates run out, daughters can be wed to the Qur'an. Such marriages are frowned upon by mainstream Islam so they are performed secretly—even most Pakistanis are unaware of the bizarre practice.

The girls involved may be only 10 or 15 years old, but the ceremony remains binding for the rest of their lives. The "bride" is afterwards kept in seclusion, contact forbidden with any male over 14 years old, including immediate family members. In some cases she is not even allowed to see a man on TV.

Husbandless wives like these may try to fill the endless hours by studying the Qur'an. Small wonder that some of the brides— estimated to number about 3,000—eventually go mad.

In the book, *Why I Am Not A Muslim*, author Ibn Warraq quotes one woman relegated to this fate: "I wish I had been born when the Arabs buried their daughters alive. Even that would have been better than this torture."

BRIDE SELLING

China's "one child" policy, which encourages the choosing of boys over girls, has led to a severely unbalanced male to female ratio. Millions of marriageable men cannot find wives. Criminal gangs and marriage brokers—essentially slave dealers —search the countryside, kidnapping and buying women and girls to offer to prospective husbands. Other women cooperate with marriage brokers in the hope of saving their families from hunger. Chinese authorities have freed an average of 8,000 kidnapped women and girls every year since 1990. But kidnapping continues to grow as a multi-million dollar industry. [4]

Thousands of young women are also trafficked *into* China to marry strangers, from Burma and other nearby countries. Smuggled brides can be sold for between $4,500 and $7,500. China's Ministry of Public Security said it rescued and repatriated 1,281 abducted foreign women in 2012.

Other countries are also engaged in the marriage trade. Burmese girls are sent over the border to wed men in Thailand, Malaysia and Singapore. Vietnamese girls are commonly trafficked to Taiwan, South Korea and Singapore.

MAIL ORDER BRIDES

Search the subject *"mail order brides"* on the Internet and you will find thousands of sites offering e-brides. And no wonder—this is a highly profitable business. Some brokers specialize by nationalities, like Russian, Japanese, African or Latina. Others boast a "warehouse" of available women. Customers on the high end of the scale may take arranged trips to various countries and bring their brides home. While men and women have undoubtedly made happy matches this way, many thousands of women end up trapped in violently abusive relationships. An investigation has shown that a number of men who seek mail order brides have criminal records or a past history of domestic abuse. Should battered immigrant wives dare protest, husbands threaten them with deportation. Often they have language difficulties and no one to turn to for help. While this industry cannot be called "trafficking" because it is done with consent, it is largely unregulated and producing an increasing number of victims worldwide.

Protective Legislation

Australia's Migration Agents Regulation Act (MARA) requires potential brides to undergo health and criminal history checks. Criminal history checks on male sponsors are only done at the government's discretion, however, and no information as to results is given to the bride-to-be, which could put her at risk. **Canada** has a similar act but requires a check of sponsoring males and will refuse his application if he has a criminal record during the prior five years. The potential bride, who can be as young as 16, is not informed why the application is denied.

New Zealand and the **UK** have immigration acts similar to Canada's but require the bride to be at least 18 and 21, respectively. The **U.S.** government passed an International Marriage Brokers Regulation Act in 2005 that specifically addresses how to inform potential mail order brides about her sponsor's criminal past. It also requires her to sign a consent form to have her information released. The act grew out of concern that unscrupulous marriage brokers were bringing young women into the country who ended up little more than servants or sex slaves. Breaking this law is penalized by fines and prison sentences.

TEMPORARY MARRIAGES

The Shiite followers of Islam (the majority of whom live in **Iran**) are allowed a unique form of marriage that may last from a few minutes to as long as 99 years. In most cases the *"nika mut'a"* arrangement is simply legalized prostitution. A man and woman sign a contract to come together for a specified time. Usually the man agrees to provide some financial benefit. The contract is then recorded and sanctioned by a cleric. Men may take as many temporary wives as they like and end the arrangement whenever they choose. A woman, however, may not end the arrangement and she may only have one husband at a time, in order to establish parentage in case she becomes pregnant. Any child born from such a union will be raised by the man and his permanent wife.

Although this practice is forbidden among Sunni Muslims, it has official religious approval among Shias and it is not considered sinful; therefore nobody has to have a guilty conscience. Temporary marriages are quite normal in Iran; young men are even counselled to regard it as an outlet for their sexual urges until the time they are ready to establish a permanent marriage. In Iraq, the practice was banned under Saddam Hussein but has now returned. It also exists in Saudi Arabia and Egypt, and is becoming increasingly popular among Muslim communities in the West.

Clerics who support temporary marriages say they offer women sexual and financial freedom. Poor families, however, only agree to such marriages out of poverty, not choice, including thousands of widows in Iraq and Iran. Although they are ashamed to participate they accept the arrangement as the only way to survive.

ACTION STEPS

- More specific legislation is needed to reduce the likelihood of these women falling into abusive and exploitative situations. Write to the law-makers in your country and encourage them to introduce or improve such measures.

- Female infanticide and gendercide will continue to create a shortage of marriageable women in some places and this, in turn, will give impetus to the trafficking industry. Raise awareness of this root cause of trafficking and join lobbying efforts of groups like those listed under "Female Infanticide" in Appendix 2, by signing petitions and writing letters.

"Is it nothing to you, all you who pass by?" Lamentations 1:12

(Endnotes)
1 http://articles.timesofindia.indiatimes.com/2012-01-27/india/30670050_1_dowry-death-harassment-and-cruelty-section-498a
2 http://www.ipsnews.net/2012/10/violence-against-women-persists-in-bangladesh/
3 http://www.dailytimes.com.pk/default.asp?page=2007\03\13\story_13-3-2007_pg12_10
4 http://85.21.179.94/publications/interns/IOM%20Report%20Heggs%20Russian%20Mail-Order%20Brides.pdf

SOS: Child Labor

At least 215 million of the world's children are illegally compelled to work for a living, and almost half of them are subjected to hazardous conditions. 152 million workers are only 5 to 14 years old. The Child Labor Index and map[1] rates 68 countries as having "extreme risk" for children, with Bangladesh, China, India, Nigeria and Pakistan among those with the most widespread abuses of child labor.

A majority of children, some 60 million, work in the agriculture sector, with only one in five paid a wage. Another 14 million are in manufacturing, many of them working in small sweatshops, home industries and brick kilns. Poverty is directly linked to child labor: The International Labour Organization (ILO) reports that the labor force participation rate of children aged 10-14 is at 30 to 60% in countries with a per capita income of US$500 or less. It also estimates that about 5.7 million children are forced into bonded labor, to pay back loans their families have taken out for basic necessities.

Little girls are particularly sought in some areas because they can be paid less than anyone. Domestic service is the largest and most hidden employer of underage girls worldwide. It is also one of the most hazardous sectors as they are exposed to physical abuse. Many girls work over 12 hours a day, seven days a week for a fraction of the minimum wage.

AFRICA

Sub-Saharan Africa has the highest incidence of child labor; in fact, numbers have increased in recent years to one in four children who are aged five to 17 working. In all of Africa, about two out of five children earn some kind of income.

- *Morocco's "Little Maids":* Although the practice is technically illegal, an estimated 23,000 small girls are annually sent from the countryside to work as domestic servants in private homes, in Casablanca alone. The ILO estimates there are a total of *50,000* girls in service all over Morocco—some as young as five and six. These children often become targets for abuse, made to labor 13 to 15 hours a day, seven days a week; sleeping on the floor and eating only leftovers. Many are forced to work even when they are ill. Some girls have been chained up when their employers go away for the weekend. Others have been starved to death, burned with irons or raped and thrown on the streets when they become pregnant. The small amount of pay they earn goes to their fathers. Although a collective was formed in 2009 to eradicate "little maids" and put girls under age 15 into school, the practice still widely continues.[2]

- *Mali:* An estimated 20,000 to 40,000 children as young as six are involved in digging shafts for artisanal gold mining, working in tunnels, hauling rocks and using toxic chemicals like mercury to separate gold and ore. Most work an average of over nine hours a day, six days a week with little or no pay.[3]

- *West Africa: Children as young as three years old are being exploited as domestic and agricultural workers in several countries. About two million children are cultivating cocoa crops, many of them trafficked for the purpose. Some parents sell their offspring to Arab Gulf states, Lebanon and Europe. Other children—many of them orphans—are lured by traffickers who promise quality schooling and vocational training abroad. Instead they are treated as virtual slaves.most endure beatings and psychological abuse, including death threats and warnings they will never see their parents again. Girls who escape sleep on the street, knock on the doors of churches or accept invitations to the homes of strangers. Some are driven into prostitution and become victims of AIDS.* [4]

- *Ivory Coast:* This country supplies 40% of the world's chocolate. UNICEF estimates that nearly half a million children aged 10 to 14, most from neighboring countries like Mali and Togo, are sold to cocoa plantations. Made to slave long hours, they are paid nothing, fed little and beaten if they attempt to escape.[5]

> **ACTION STEP:** *Get involved in the International Labor Rights Forum's "Cocoa Campaign" to combat forced child labor in the billion-dollar cocoa industry.*
> *www.laborrights.org/stop-child-labor/cocoa-campaign*

Malawi: This country has the highest incidence of child laborers in Southern Africa, according to the FAFO Institute for Applied Social Science. A shocking 78% of children between the ages of 10 to 14 and 55% of seven to nine year olds (an estimated total of 78,000) work full or part-time with their parents on tobacco farms, up to 12 hours a day. Many suffer severe symptoms because they go without protective clothing and absorb too much nicotine.[6]

SOUTH ASIA

Despite laws prohibiting the practice, child labor is rampant within South Asia's handmade rug industry. Some 250,000 children aged 4 to 14 have been kidnapped or sold and forced to work as many as 18 hours a day to weave rugs destined for export markets in Europe and the US.

ACTION STEP: When buying a new rug, look for a GoodWeave label. GoodWeave International is a non-governmental organization working to end child labor in the handmade rug industry and offer educational opportunities to children in South Asia. Support retailers of GoodWeave label products.[7]

- **Bangladesh:** Almost a third of this country's workforce are children, according to UNICEF. About 4.7 million are aged 5 to 14 and 1.3 million are working in hazardous conditions.[8] One survey found that almost 70 per cent of girls involved in domestic service in Bangladesh experienced physical abuse and systematic beatings.[9] A major garment factory fire killing over 1,100 workers near Dhaka captured world headlines in 2013. More than 3 million Bangladeshis work in the garment industry and 90% of these workers are women and girls.

- **India:** Home to one-fifth of the world's child population, this nation also has the largest child workforce. Since they require only a fraction of the salary paid adults, children take a significant role in the manufacture of beedi [small cigarettes], matches, jewelry, carpet and cotton rope making, domestic work, quarrying, mining and farming. Around 400,000 are working on India's cotton seed farms. Reliable agencies estimate between **12 and 50 million** children under age 14 are working. And although all bonded labor and servitude was officially abolished in 1975, at least 15 million children today are "bonded" to creditors to pay back family debts. Many boys and girls are abused or made ill by harmful conditions or exposure to chemicals. Poor pay and inflated interest rates make it almost impossible for loans to be repaid.[10] Although new legislation is being passed, like the Child and Adolescent Labor (Prohibition) Bill, its effectiveness will depend on the level of enforcement.

"My sister is ten years old. Every morning at seven she goes to the bonded labor man, and every night at nine she comes home. He treats her badly; he hits her if he thinks she is working slowly or if she talks to the other children, he yells at her, he comes looking for her if she is sick and cannot go to work….. I don't care about school or playing. I don't care about any of that. All I want is to bring my sister home from the bonded labor man. For 600 rupees I can bring her home—that is our only chance to get her back. We don't have 600 rupees . . . we will never have 600 rupees."[11] —Lakshmi, nine year-old cigarette roller in Tamil Nadu, India. 600 rupees was then the equivalent of approximately $17. 50

- *Pakistan: While the last government survey in 1996 said that 3.3 million children aged 5-14 were workers, UNICEF estimates that today's more accurate figure is at least 10 million,* with at least eight million of them under age 15. Debt bondage enslaves the greatest numbers. Even though bonded labor has been a punishable offence since 1992, few employers have ever been prosecuted for breaking the law.

- *Afghanistan:* According to UNICEF, poverty forces one in three school-age children to work. Around half the workforce in Afghanistan's brick kilns is under 14.

EAST ASIA/PACIFIC

The highest total of child workers (113.6 million) live in the Asia Pacific area.

A "procurer" typically promises destitute parents they will give their children a good job and education in the city. Other children are kidnapped to work in factories and sweat shops. Most receive no pay and are confined in squalid living conditions, beaten with sticks and iron rods and not allowed to see their parents. Children have been discovered branded with red hot irons, burned with cigarettes, starved, whipped, beaten while hanging upside down, chained up, abused in an intimate way, and kept locked in cupboards for days on end.[12]

- *Cambodia:* Over half of the child population between seven and 15 are part of the workforce. Although protective legislation exists, it is weak and often ignored.

- *Philippines:* According to a 2011 report by the International Labour Organization, 6.5 million children go to work in this country. As many as three million are subjected to environments that are considered hazardous for up to 16 hours a day. These young laborers, some under the age of seven, are compelled to support their families by farming, mining, fishing, factory work, domestic service and sex tourism.[13]

- *Indonesia:* About 690,000 underage girls are employed as domestic help, often forced to work up to 18 hours a day for, in some cases, as little as six cents an hour or no pay at all and no day off. In the worst cases, the children are physically, psychologically or sexually abused. [Human Rights Watch Report, 2009]

- *Australia:* New South Wales has no minimum working age, and employment of children is regulated only in certain industries. The Fair Wear Campaign estimates that 50-70% of Australian-made clothing is outsourced, usually to migrant women and their children working at home or in backyard sweatshops in suburbs around Australian cities. Tens of thousands work in poor conditions for very little pay, exposed to hazards that lead to serious injuries and deaths each year.

EUROPE, CENTRAL ASIA, MIDDLE EAST

- *Roma* (gypsy) children are particularly vulnerable to forced labor in many areas of Europe, since 80% live in poverty. Thousands of **Albania's Roma** girls and boys, for instance, are sent to **Italy** and **Greece** in order to earn money for their adult "masters" by begging and cleaning shoes or car windows. [See also "Vital Statistics: Trafficking"]

- In *Central Asia and the Caucasus,* many street children fall victim to the worst forms of labor. Children in rural parts are frequently trafficked to urban areas and other countries for exploitation. Migrant labor is also common. The Human Rights Watch has documented illegal labor by children as young as 10 on **Kazakhstan's** tobacco farms. Along with their parents they face wage violations, debt bondage, excessively long working hours, exposure to pesticides and lack of clean drinking water. The Cotton Campaign coalition [http://www.cottoncampaign.org] with other human rights defenders has long drawn attention to **Uzbekistan's** use of over a million adult and child forced laborers to work its cotton fields.

- *Iraq:* Almost one in three of this country's 15 million children has lost a parent through the war. 700,000 are not attending primary school and around 800,000 children between the ages of five and 14 are working.

CENTRAL & SOUTH AMERICA

Seven percent of the world's child workers between the ages of five and 14 live in Latin America. One in six children are wage earners. More than two million are being sexually exploited as a growing number of sex tourists head to Central America.

Guatemala has the highest incidence of child labor in Latin America. The official minimum working age is 14 but many below that age are among the one million-plus children who are expected to contribute to the family income.

- **MINING:** Children are commonly put to use in small-scale gold, silver and other mining operations in Latin America. Exposure to toxins and dangerous conditions often leads to skin and lung disorders as well as causing damage to growing bones and organs. Up to 65,000 children are involved in Bolivia, Ecuador and Peru alone.

- **BANANA PLANTATIONS:** Although progress has been made in reducing the hundreds of thousands of children working on banana plantations the problem still exists, particularly in Ecuador which is the largest exporter. Besides missing school, these children work up to 12 hours a day and are exposed to pesticides and knife accidents.

Action Step:
Find out more about BananaLink.org.uk, working for the benefit of banana and pineapple plantation workers.

NORTH AMERICA

Canada: In British Columbia, a child can go to work at age 12 anywhere except in mines, taverns, bars and lounges, and work any time of the day or night except during school hours. The province actually lowered its child labor age to 12 in 2003; since then there has been a 10-fold increase in the number of child workplace injury claims.[14] A campaign has been underway for several years to overthrow British Colombia's neglectful child labor laws.

USA: 800,000 migrant children travel with their families to all parts of the United States to work on industrial farms. Though as young as seven or eight, they may toil as many as 12 to 16 hours per day and often miss months of schooling. Experts estimate as many as 65% end up dropping out of school. Living conditions are often poor and pesticide exposure can cause skin irritations and breathing difficulties.

In addition to American-born children, many others are trafficked into the U.S. from other countries by professional smugglers. In 2010, more than 8,000 unaccompanied immigrant children were taken into custody at borders and airports by U.S. immigration authorities. The U.S. Department of Justice estimates that between 100,000 and three million children are being sexually exploited in exchange for money, drugs, food or shelter.

As of 2013 the United States and Somalia are the only UN member nations that have not yet ratified the Convention of the Rights of the Child (CRC), which was adopted in 1989. The CRC has four key themes: the right of children to survival; to develop to their fullest potential; to protection from abuse, neglect and exploitation; and to participate in family, cultural and social life.

Action Steps

- Check the websites listed under "Child Labor" in Appendix 2 for other campaigns you can support.

- Get children and families you know to observe the annual "World Day Against Child Labour" on June 12th to highlight the plight of exploited children.

"Arise, cry out in the night...pour out your heart like water in the presence of the Lord. Lift up your hands to him for the lives of your children, who faint from hunger at the head of every street."
Lamentations 2:19

(Endnotes)
1 http://maplecroft.com/about/news/child-labor-index.html
2 http://www.alarabiya.net/articles/2012/05/29/217283.html; http://www.moroccoworldnews.com/2013/01/75104/child-housemaids-in-morocco-as-unstoppable-as-the-wind-4/
3 http://educationenvoy.org/child_labor_and_education_US.pdf
4 http://thecnnfreedomproject.blogs.cnn.com/2012/01/19/child-slavery-and-chocolate- all-too-easy-to-find/
5 http://www.laborrights.org/stop-child-labor/tobacco-campaign
6 http://www.goodweave.org/about/rug_certification_label
7 http://www.unicef.org/bangladesh/Child_labour.pdf
8 http://educationenvoy.org/child_labor_and_education_US.pdf
9 http://www.dalitfreedom.org.au/trafficking/bonded-labour.html
10 http://www.hrw.org/reports/1996/India3.htm
12 http://www.anti-slaverysociety.addr.com/slaverysasia.htm
13 http://www.childfund.org/child-labor-in-the-philippines/
14 http://www.theglobeandmail.com/commentary/bcs-child-labour-laws-are-the-most-neglectful-in-the-world/article627018/

SOS: Child Marriages

Every day approximately 25,000 underage girls are forced into marriage. One in every seven girls in developing countries is married off before the age of 15. More than 60 million girls worldwide are married before they turn 18.

In countries like Niger, Chad, Mali, Bangladesh, Guinea and the Central African Republic, the rate of early and forced marriage is 60 percent and over. Child brides are also particularly common in South Asia (46 percent of girls) and in sub-Saharan Africa (38 percent).[1] Yet girls are forced into marriage in Western nations as well.

Why do underage and forced marriages happen?

Global children's charity Plan says that parents who force their girls to marry without their consent are largely driven by poverty, gender inequality, negative traditional or religious practices, failure to enforce laws and emergencies or conflicts.[2] According to the organization End Child Prostitution, Pornography and Trafficking of Children for Sexual Purposes (ECPAT), child marriages can also be a thinly-veiled form of sex tourism, particularly in the Middle East and South Asia. A man travels to another country and marries a young girl in exchange for money or other benefits to the parents. After spending a week with her he then returns home, never to interact with the girl or family again. In other cases a tourist marries or promises to marry an underage girl, then brings her back to his country. The victim is then used for continual sexual exploitation as she is young and totally dependent on him.[3]

What are the consequences?

Young brides are usually forced to drop out of school, contributing to illiteracy and ignorance. They are also more likely to experience forced sexual relations and violence from older husbands. This can result in poor reproductive health.

Leading cause of maternal mortality

Underage girls are not physically ready to give birth. According to the World Health Organization, pregnancy-related deaths are the leading cause of death for girls 15 to 19 years old. An estimated 70,000 girls under 15 die each year from complications during pregnancy or childbirth, a mortality rate 25 times higher than the norm. The mortality rate is twice as high for 15 to 19-year-olds. Miscarriages, stillbirths and complications like fistulas are also much more likely.

INTO THE MUSLIM WORLD

Around many parts of the Muslim world, even in Europe and the Americas, it is not uncommon for girls as young as nine to be married to men old enough to be their grandfathers. While the practice may be officially illegal, it is accepted because the Prophet Muhammad himself set the precedent. At the age of 52 he took a six-year-old child as one of his wives; the marriage was sexually consummated when she was nine.

In 2011 a prominent cleric and member of Saudi Arabia's highest religious council, Dr. Salih bin Fawzan, made headlines when he issued a *fatwa* (legal ruling) that asserted there is no minimum age for marriage. Girls could be married "even if they are in the cradle."[4]

Afghanistan: As many as 80 percent of marriages in Afghanistan take place without the consent of the bride, who is often a child. The brutal death of a 14-year-old girl made headlines in December 2012. Two brothers cut Gastina's throat after her father, Noor Rahman, refused to agree to her marriage on the grounds that she was too young. Many girls have decided that killing themselves is the only way out.[5] Suicide attempts such as jumping off buildings, self-immolations and drinking poison have increased among girls who are being forced to marry against their will.

Iran: In 2012 Iranian lawmakers announced a decision to allow nine-year-olds the opportunity to marry, calling the legal minimum age of 13 "un-Islamic." The number of brides under 10 years of age is sharply rising. There are an estimated 50 million child brides in Iran.[6]

Bangladesh: The legal ban on the marriage of girls below 18 years of age has rarely been enforced. Up to 66 percent of girls in Bangladesh are married before their 18th birthday and 20 percent are wed before their 15th birthday. Some brides are just 10 years old.

Malaysia: The Minister of Legal Affairs has ruled that girls below the age of 16 are allowed to marry as long as permission is obtained from Islamic religious courts.

Morocco: In 2012 the BBC reported the case of a 16-year-old girl who swallowed rat poison after a forced marriage to the man who kidnapped and raped her. The country's penal code does not prosecute men who kidnap minors in order to marry them.[7]

Nigeria: Most of the Muslim North has resisted the country's Child's Rights Act which protects underage girls. According to the British Council in Nigeria, more than half of Nigerian women in the North are married by the age of 16 and are expected to give birth to a child during the first year of marriage.

Ethiopia: Girls in rural areas have been known to be married off at the age of eight, their families disregarding a federal law that states the legal age is 18. Forty-eight percent are married before the age of 15. Abduction of women, although a criminal offence, is still considered as a legitimate way of procuring a bride, especially in the South.

Hunger Brides

2012 saw an increase in "drought" or "hunger brides" in the famine-stricken countries of West Africa's Sahel region and the Horn of Africa in the East. Parents unable to feed their children have been selling young daughters in marriage as a survival strategy, for as little as $170. This is happening in Niger, where even during the best of times one in three girls is married by the time she is 15, and Ethiopia, Kenya and Somalia. The younger the girl, the better the deal.

Pakistan: The most widespread crime against females in Pakistan is forced marriage, says a report of the NGO coalition "Free and Fair Election Pakistan." Almost 68 percent of Pakistan's population resides in rural areas, and many girls in the 12 to 14 age group are either pregnant or already mothers. To circumvent the law, parents record their daughter's age as 16 on the marriage certificate. Since a birth certificate is not yet a legal requirement for marriages in Pakistan, there is no way to check falsification of age.[8]

Pakistan's "Marriage Act"

A law passed under the military dictatorship of Zia ul-Haq in 1985 rules that if a non-Muslim woman converts to Islam, her previous marriage is null and void. Some Muslims regard this law as an invitation to kidnap, rape and bully Christian women and girls into converting to Islam. They are part of the "spoils of war." The victims— an estimated 700 girls each year—are then forced to marry their Muslim captors, who claim that their parents and husbands have lost all rights to the abducted women and girls. Through indifference, agreement or fear, most local police simply go along with it.[9]

Nazir Bhatti, president of the Pakistan Christian Congress, has stated that over 99.9 percent of rape cases involving Christian women go unreported, as reporting an assault would bring shame to their families and keep them from finding a husband.

INTO THE HINDU WORLD

India: India has the largest number of child brides in the world, according to the United Nations Population Fund (UNFPA) in 2013. Although Indian law sets 18 as the minimum age for a woman to marry, 47 percent are wed below that age.[10] The UNFPA has also projected that of the 140 million girls who will be married under 18 by 2020, 50 million will be under the age of 15.[11] In northern states like eastern Uttar Pradesh, girls are often as young as a few months to eight years when they are wed. The brides remain in their maternal homes until they attain puberty; then they are dispatched to their marital homes.

In a landmark decision in Rajasthan in 2012, the marriage that had taken place 17 years before between a one-year-old baby girl and three-year-old boy was annulled. Early marriages are common in this state, and not all grooms' families are prepared to wait for puberty. The Hindu Akshaya Tritiya festival each April or May is a traditional date for mass child weddings,[12] in spite of the Indian government's opposition. In many cases documented by sociologists, girls as young as six or seven have been taken away by their husbands' families to begin working as servants or field hands. Many husbands reportedly tire of their marriages after the birth of their third, fourth or fifth child, when their wives are still teenagers.

Nepal: Over 34 percent of new marriages in this Himalayan nation involve brides under 15 years of age despite a ban on the practice, according to the Ministry of Women, Children and Social Welfare. If the girl is particularly young, nuptials between the families are routinely undertaken in secret because a lower dowry is paid. The younger the bride is, the cheaper the amount that their families have to provide. Although it is illegal it is not uncommon for Nepali men, especially in rural areas, to take two or even three wives. More than 240,000 children do not attend school in Nepal according to government figures, and officials believe most of them are girls, especially those who were married at a young age.[13]

INTO THE WESTERN WORLD

▶ *USA:* The Fundamentalist Church of Jesus Christ of Latter Day Saints (FLDS) is a sect that broke from the Mormon Church 70 years ago in bitter disagreement about the practice of plural marriage, polygamy and underage brides as young as 14. Between 6 - 10,000 followers live in six states. The FLDS teaches that the only way a man can reach the highest level of heaven is to take at least three wives in this life. Even though polygamy is against the law in Utah and unconstitutional in Arizona, FLDS members have never made a secret of their lifestyle. The most widely accepted estimate—made by Kathryn Daynes, a Brigham Young University professor, and other experts—is that the U.S. has between 30,000 and 50,000 polygamists.[14] The Tahirih Justice Foundation has also identified 3,000 cases of forced marriage in the U.S. during the last two years. Many of the victims were immigrants from Muslim countries, but the survey found victims from Hindu, Buddhist and Christian (primarily Mexican Catholic) backgrounds.

Europe: Norway, Denmark, Germany, Austria, Malta, Belgium and Cyprus have passed laws that criminalize forced marriage. Yet well over a dozen countries have established 14 or 15 as the age of consent for sexual intercourse. Only in 2013 did Spain raised its minimum marriage age from 14.

In the **United Kingdom,** Forced Marriage Protection Orders were introduced in 2008 and the British government announced plans to follow the lead of several other European countries in making such marriages a criminal offence, perhaps in 2013 or 2014. The Forced Marriage Unit intervened to help 400 children in 2011 and 250 in 2012, including a two-year-old. The unit also gave advice or support in another 1,485 cases;[15] yet research carried out by the Department for Children, Schools and Families estimated that nationally the number of reported cases of forced marriage in England was between 5,000 and 8,000. Underage marriages often take place "underground" and many girls are taken to other countries to be wed.

Australia & New Zealand: New South Wales Commissioner for Women Pru Goward suggested in 2012 that there were around 1,000 cases of forced marriage or sex slavery each year in Australia. In New Zealand, too, many such marriages are known to be quietly carried out, especially in immigrant communities.

Authorities in the West are often reluctant to intervene in cases of forced marriage; they view them as a cultural issue and fear a backlash from powerful minority factions.

Action Steps

Girls Not Brides is a global partnership committed to ending the harmful traditional practice of child marriage. Check out the website, www.girlsnotbrides.org. Global charity Plan also has a petition against early and forced marriages: www.plan-uk.org. Think about joining the Equality Action Network to get alerts and updates about campaigns: www.equalitynow.org.

(Endnotes)
1   http://www.plan-uk.org/early-and-forced-marriage
2   Ibid.
3   http://www.ecpat.net/ei/Publications/CST/CST_FAQ_ENG.pdf
4   http://forum09.faithfreedom.org/viewtopic.php?f=4&t=10258
5   http://world.myjoyonline.com/pages/news/201304/104829.php
6   http://frontpagemag.com/2012/frank-crimi/iranian-child-brides-get-younger-and-more-numerous/
7   http://www.bbc.co.uk/news/world-africa-17416426
8   http://www.girlsnotbrides.org/national-marriage-registration-to-enforce-child-marriage-laws-in-pakistan/
9   http://www.christianfreedom.org/the-christian-winter/persecution-in-pakistan/
10 http://www.hindustantimes.com/India-news/NewDelhi/India-leading-world-s-child-marriages-UN/Article1-1023307.aspx
11 http://www.cbn.com/cbnnews/world/2012/June/Innocence-Lost-Indias-Children-Marrying-at-Age-8/
12 http://www.raonline.ch/pages/np/npwom05.html
13 http://www.hcn.org/issues/44.10/flds-continues-abusive-polygamist-practices-in-utah-and-arizona
14 http://www.tahirih.org/site/wp-content/uploads/2011/09/REPORT-Tahirih-Survey-on-Forced-Marriage-in-Immigrant-Communities-in-the-United-States-September-2011.pdf
15 http://www.guardian.co.uk/world/2013/mar/05/two-year-old-forced-marriage-risk

SOS: Childbirth

Globally, more than 500,000 women every year—an average of over 1,300 per day—lose their lives because of complications related to pregnancy or childbirth. Yet 90% of these deaths are preventable.

A Save the Children "State of the World's Mothers" report in 2013 named 10 African countries as the worst places to be a mother, based on a number of factors regarding their health and well-being. At the bottom of the list was the Democratic Republic of the Congo, followed by Somalia, Sierra Leone, Mali, Niger, Central African Republic, Gambia, Nigeria, Chad and Ivory Coast. The best places were, first, Finland, then Sweden, Norway, Iceland, Netherlands, Denmark, Spain, Belgium, Germany and Australia. **Over a million children each year die on the day they are born.**

Women living in developing countries are 97 times more likely to die during pregnancy or childbirth than women in first-world countries. While only one in over 17,000 women in Sweden, for instance, risk maternal death during their lifetime, in West and Central Africa the ratio is one in 26. In Bangladesh it's one in 51. Guatemala has the highest maternal death rate in Latin America, with one in 71 women dying. [WHO/UNICEF/WORLD BANK]

Over 90% of people alive today were born at home. Fewer than 6 in 10 women in the developing world give birth with the benefit of a skilled professional, such as a midwife or doctor, in attendance. Many simply don't have the money to pay for giving birth in a clinic or hospital, even if a medical facility exists.

➢ "Maternal death" is the death of a woman while she is pregnant or within 42 days of termination of pregnancy. As few as five percent of women receive care during this period in very poor countries and regions, yet according to WHO, two-thirds of maternal and newborn deaths occur in the first two days after delivery. By contrast, virtually all new mothers in developed countries receive postpartum care.

- Hemorrhage is the leading cause of death during pregnancy and childbirth, accounting for one-third of maternal mortality. This is followed by infections, unsafe abortions, obstructed labor and disorders related to high blood pressure.

- Giving birth is the number one killer of teenagers across the world. Sixteen million adolescent girls become mothers every year.[1] One in five give birth before they're 18, and they are five times more likely to die. Their infants are also 60% more likely to die.

- Poor nutrition of mothers-to-be is often a contributing factor to maternal death. [See notes under "Vital Statistics: Health and Life Expectancy"]

- Even the lack of simple hygiene can be lethal. A recent study shows that handwashing with soap by birth attendants and mothers significantly increases newborn survival rates by up to 44 percent.

COMPLICATIONS

For every woman who dies, approximately 20 others *(or a total of 10 to 15 million women each year)* develop infections or serious complications that leave humiliating, painful and long-term infections, injuries and disabilities.[2]

Obstructed Labor

One frequent complication is the inability of the fetus to descend through the birth canal because of some barrier, in spite of uterine contractions. A factor contributing to the high incidence of this condition in the developing world is early marriage. Girls aged 10 or younger have a birth canal that is too small. This can result in permanent nerve damage and muscle deterioration in the feet and legs. Those worst affected become crippled.

In some parts of Arab West Africa, midwives sometimes insert a long knife into an overly narrow vagina in order to widen it for birth. The cut they make can cause terrible damage. Sometimes the knife is inserted down the urethra to make the cut, laying bare the entire lower urinary tract. Many women die immediately from hemorrhage.

Fistula

An estimated two million women in Asia and sub-Saharan Africa live with untreated obstetric fistula, according to the Fistula Foundation. This condition can occur after they have endured long days of agonizing, obstructed labor and given birth to a stillborn child. Fistula is a hole between the vaginal wall and rectum or bladder that results in total, permanent incontinence—unless the woman can get surgical repair. Few can afford it, even if their remote village offers the option.

The shame of living with the continuous filth and smell that such a condition imposes is bad enough, but folklore in some areas judges obstetric fistula to be the result of marital infidelity or sexually transmitted disease. Girls and young women suffering from fistulas are therefore ostracized by their communities and abandoned by their families. Many must beg to stay alive.

A cleansing ritual practiced by some African cultures can also cause fistula. For 40 days following childbirth, a friend or relative pours a solution containing potash into the mother's vagina. If the solution is improperly made the alkaline causes chemical destruction of the vaginal tissue, and a fistula develops.

Sadly, a simple, low-cost operation is all that it would take to restore these thousands of cast-off women to normal lives.

Action Step

Support the work of The Fistula Foundation, the Freedom from Fistula Foundation and other groups mentioned in Appendix 2 that are trying to address this critical need in many countries.

(Endnotes)
1 http://www.unfpa.org/public/adolescents
2 http://www.factsforlifeglobal.org/01/1.html

SOS: Disabled Women

The Hearing Impaired

- Roughly one person in every 1000 on our planet has a moderate to severe hearing impediment—an estimated 554 million men, women and children.

- 35.5 million are officially deaf.

- About half of all cases could be prevented.

- More than two-thirds of those affected live in the developing world, and 80% of these people have no access to education.

- About 70 million deaf people use sign language as their first language or mother tongue.

The deaf are the 4th largest people group in the world who are unreached with the gospel. For a country-by-country list of the globe's unreached deaf people groups, check out the Joshua Project [www. joshuaproject.net]. The deaf are listed as a "least reached" population group in 30 countries.

▶*90% of deaf individuals have hearing parents. Only about one in 10 of these parents can communicate with their child using sign language. In some countries it is also forbidden to use sign language even in school classrooms.*

▶Each country has one or more sign languages. The adoption of a universal sign language such as International Sign (IS) would greatly expedite the production and sharing of resources, but the majority of people have yet to learn it.

▶Current hearing aid production meets less than 10% of the world's need, according to the World Health Organization.

▶**USA:** The deaf community are listed by several missions as the **largest** unreached people group in America, with 23 million individuals having some form of hearing loss. The native language of deaf people here, American Sign Language (ASL), is the **third most used language** in North America. **Fewer than eight out of every 100** deaf people in the U.S. ever attend church. **Fewer than four out of 100** claim a personal relationship with Christ.

▶**China's** deaf population, numbering around 72 million, could be classed as China's largest minority people group.[1] They live in every city, every township and thousands of small villages. About one million of China's 1.6 million deaf children became deaf through inappropriate use of antibiotics.[2]

Special Problems of Abused Deaf Women:

• Dealing with police, court systems, shelters, and other support services is more problematic because comparatively few people understand sign language.

• Deaf women often suffer job discrimination, with higher unemployment rates and lower salaries.

• Economic dependency on others often leads to being trapped in abusive situations for longer periods.

• Guilt, shame and low self-esteem often influence deaf women to suffer without protest.

WOMEN AND CHILDREN WITH OTHER DISABILITIES

According to the World Bank and World Health Organization, more than one billion people in the world live with some form of disability; of this number at least 300 million are women. The amount of abuse suffered by disabled individuals is of pandemic proportions, and women are particularly vulnerable. Some countries have no laws to protect them.

• In some cultures, disabled people are considered cursed. They may be hidden away, ignored, uncared for and even allowed to die.

• Individuals with disabilities, including those who are hard of hearing, are more vulnerable to trafficking and exploitation by forced labor.

• Article 24 of The International Convention on the Rights of Persons with Disabilities maintains the right to education, yet 16 million children with disabilities are not in school—one-fourth of them are blind. Some consider educating such children a waste of money. Girls in particular are excluded.

• Disabled women are two to five times more likely to be abused than non-disabled women, depending on whether they live in a community or in an institution. They are also likely to experience abuse over a longer period of time and suffer more severe injuries.

Institutional Abuse

According to Hesperian Health Guides, examples of mistreatment in institutions are:

- forced sex with workers, caretakers, or other residents
- being beaten, slapped, or hurt
- forced sterilization or abortions
- being locked in a room alone
- ice baths or cold showers as punishment
- forced medication (tranquilizers)
- having to undress or be naked in front of other people
- watching other people be abused or hurt
- being tied down or put in restraints

At Home

Even in their homes, abuse of disabled individuals can take the form of neglect, such as withholding food or care; physical or sexual assault or rough handling or over-medication; psychological abuse such as verbal intimidation and threats, and emotional deprivation and isolation. They may also be the victims of financial exploitation as others misuse their rightful resources. [Disabled Women's Network Ontario]

Sterilization

Women with disabilities are particularly vulnerable to forced sterilizations that render them incapable of sexual reproduction. These may be performed under the auspices of legitimate medical care or the consent of others in their name, supposedly in the woman's "best interests." But sterilization is an irreversible medical procedure with profound physical and psychological effects.[3] Eugenics programs to improve society by curtailing the reproductive capability of people considered mentally or physically deficient through forced sterilizations were quite common during the years preceding World War II, especially in **Northern Europe.** In some countries, such as **Sweden** and **Canada,** programs lasted into the 1970's.[4] More recently in **India**, forced hysterectomies were conducted on several mentally challenged women between 18 and 35 years of age at the Sassoon General Hospital in Pune, in 1994, because they were incapable of maintaining menstrual hygiene and hospital staff found it a strain on their resources and time.[5] In **Australia**, as in many other countries, parents of girls with disabilities can apply for court orders to allow the involuntarily sterilization of their child, even a girl as young as 11 as happened in 2013.[6] It is unknown how many such violations of human rights are quietly carried out worldwide.

▶Women with mental disorders face disproportionately more risk factors than men, including gender based violence, socioeconomic disadvantage, low income and income inequality and low or subordinate social status and rank. [World Health Organization]

Triple Jeopardy for Females

▶In countries where the birth of female children is not so welcome and where female feticide is rampant, like India, a disabled girl-child or woman is at the receiving end of even more contempt and neglect. A study by human rights group CREA of women in India, Bangladesh and Nepal showed that disabled women experience regular and ongoing discrimination within society.[7] A "Triple Jeopardy" research project in Cambodia, released by AusAID in 2013, points to the interplay between gender inequality, disability and poverty that magnifies the disadvantages faced by women with disability.[8] And in Africa, where the myth exists that having sex with a virgin can cure a person of HIV or AIDS, women and girls with disabilities are targeted for rape because they are presumed to be asexual and thus virgins.[9]

Mentally and physically disabled women are among the most discriminated-against and at-risk people groups in our societies, often treated as asexual or even "invisible."

The UN Convention on the Rights of Persons with Disabilities (UNCRPD) is the first human rights treaty of the 21st Century. Coming into force in 2008, this reaffirmed disabled people's rights and signalled a further major step in disabled people's journey to becoming full and equal citizens. So far, 155 member nations have signed.

Action Steps

Support December 3, the International Day of People with Disability. Make it a focus of your church or interest group and use it as a springboard for reaching out to marginalized members of your community. Try doing a fundraiser for a project to help the disabled, either at home or abroad.

Scorn has broken my heart and has left me helpless; I looked for sympathy, but there was none, for comforters, but I found none. Psalm 69:20

(Endnotes)
1 http://www.heartsandhandschina.com/
2 http://news.xinhuanet.com/english2010/health/2011-02/10/c_13725709.htm
3 http://www.hrw.org/news/2011/11/10/sterilization-women-and-girls-disabilities
4 http://en.wikipedia.org/wiki/Compulsory_sterilization
5 http://infochangeindia.org/disabilities/backgrounder/protecting-women-with-disabilities-from-violence.html
6 http://www.hrw.org/news/2013/04/16/protect-rights-women-girls-disabilities
7 http://web.creaworld.org/files/cmir.pdf
8 http://www.ausaid.gov.au/HotTopics/Pages/Display.aspx?QID=1035
9 http://www.stopvaw.org/women_with_disabilities

SOS: Domestic Violence*

Domestic violence is the most widespread form of abuse against women and children in the world today. A woman is killed by her partner or 'ex' twice each week in the UK, twice a day in Guatemala and every 35 minutes in Ukraine. One in four women will suffer domestic abuse in their lifetime. Only 44 countries specifically protect women against domestic violence.

- **USA:** Battering is the single largest cause of injury to women in the United States, aged 15-44, according to the U.S. Surgeon General: more than mugging, car accidents and rape combined. A woman is assaulted or beaten every nine seconds. Intimate partner violence leads to 16,800 homicides each year, and costs the public over $5.8 billion. 3.3 million American children also suffer abuse each year, and an estimated 10 million witness some form of domestic violence. [National Coalition Against Domestic Violence]

- **Great Britain:** More than 1.2 million British women suffered domestic violence in 2012, says the Home Office. Experts believe the actual number of incidents is closer to 13 million, since the vast majority go unreported. Seven out of 10 women sleeping rough in the country say they have escaped violence from their partners.[1] Disabled women are twice as likely to suffer abuse, and women married to Muslim men are more likely to be killed by their spouses than any other women in Britain. The UK's Crown Prosecution Service has warned that the growing number of Sharia (Islamic) courts in the country are putting women at risk of violence from abusive husbands. Their decisions sometimes run contrary to British law, and evidence exists that in some cases domestic violence has been condoned.[2]

Muslims with multiple wives may bring them to the UK when they emigrate, and a growing number of British Muslim men are taking second or third wives, even though polygamy is illegal. The wives are considered as single mothers by the welfare system, so several "families" fathered by the same man can all claim benefits. Social workers estimate the population includes at least 20,000 bigamous or polygamous marriages.

- **Sweden:** Eight out of 10 Muslim mosques were discovered by Swedish state television undercover investigators in 2012 to be telling women not to report abusive husbands, and that polygamy is sometimes acceptable.

- **Italy:** So many women are being killed by their partners or former partners that a new word has recently begun showing up in the media: *femminicidio*, meaning gender-based murders or femicide. In most cases a woman decides to leave her man (husband or boyfriend) and he kills her. According to a women's shelter in Florence, *every two days a woman is killed as a result of domestic violence*. In 2013, Italy's government unanimously ratified the Convention of the Council of Europe on "preventing and combating violence against women and domestic violence."

LATIN AMERICA and CARIBBEAN

This area has some of the highest abuse rates in the world, affecting 35-40% of women. This is partly due to a machismo culture which supports male superiority and allows their domination over females. Courts in many countries are reluctant to rule on domestic violence, considering it a family matter and not within the court's jurisdiction.

- **Bolivia** has the highest levels of domestic violence in South America, according to data collected by the UN in 2011. A new law to protect women was introduced by Bolivia's congress in 2013.[3]

- **Guatemala** ranks third in the world for the murder of women, often by abusive lovers. Few of the guilty are convicted and sentenced.[4]

- **Colombia:** In 2011, official records show 42 women in Colombia suffered acid attacks. In 2012, that number nearly quadrupled, with 150 reported acid attacks. The government spends 74 million dollars a year in assistance for mistreated women. 70% of cases are not reported.[5]

- **Mexico's** laws do not adequately protect women and girls; beating wives or children is not considered an offence, and 90% of women do not report abuses to authorities. [Human Rights Watch]

- In Sao Paulo, **Brazil**, a woman is assaulted every 15 seconds.[6]

AFRICA

Swaziland: Women in this African country are expected to remain silent when they are abused. In fact, there is a Swati word for "wife" or "woman" that means: *one who dies without speaking of what she has endured.* Swaziland has no specific law that criminalizes domestic violence; only recently has it begun drafting laws against sexual offences, and prosecuting rape cases.

Ghana: Nearly 10,000 cases of violence were reported to the Ghana police Domestic Violence Support Unit in 2012.

Uganda: A report published on the UNHCR's website, citing figures from various sources, found that 60% of men and 70% of women in Uganda condone wife beating if, for example a woman burns food or refuses sex. Although this country has finally passed a domestic violence act it had not yet been implemented in 2013. Marital rape is not a crime in Uganda.

South Africa: According to one-year statistics from the South African Police Services released in 2011/12, seven women were murdered each day. Crime trackers estimate that one woman gets raped every 17 seconds and a child is raped every three minutes, bestowing upon South Africa the dubious title of the world's rape capital, according to Interpol. Yet, less than one percent of rape cases are reported to police. [allafrica.com]

ASIA

Japan: Domestic violence has been so pervasive for so long that it is considered a normal part of marriage—and it is getting worse. Some blame the economic recession for the daily life-threatening violence, not only to women but children and old people. Statistics are inaccurate since nine out of 10 victims are unable or unwilling (out of fear or shame) to seek assistance. The number of shelters for battered women has increased but is still inadequate.

India: A kidnapping or abduction occurs every 43 minutes, a dowry death every 75 minutes, a rape every 34 minutes, an act of cruelty every 33 minutes and a criminal offence against women every seven minutes according to data compiled by women's groups.[7] Out of 15 million girls born each year, only 25% will get to reach their fifteenth birthday. A Protection of Women Against Domestic Violence Act was brought into force in 2006, but implementation is often halfhearted. Reported incidents of abuse rose by 6.5 percent in 2012 from the previous year.[8]

UNICEF reported in 2012 that 52% of India's adolescent girls and 57% of adolescent boys think it is justifiable for a man to beat his wife. According to the Nation's Crime Records Bureau there was a

7.1% hike in recorded crimes against women between 2010 and 2011. The biggest leap was in cases under the "dowry prohibition act" (up 27.7%), of kidnapping and abduction (up 19.4%) and rape (up 9.2%). [See also "Vital Statistics: Brides at Risk"]

Bangladesh: At least 174,691women in this country were the victims of violence, including acid attacks, abductions, rapes, murders, trafficking, and dowry-related violence, between 2001 and 2012, according to a report by the country's police. Tens of thousands more suffer daily beatings never reported to police. Rising physical and mental torture is evidenced by the fact that suicide is a major cause of women's death in this country. And according to the United Nations Human Development Report, Bangladesh has the worst record for rape in the region, meaning that statistically one in every 1,000 women is raped.[9]

Over 3,000 Bangladeshi women have had acid thrown in their faces in the last decade, mostly by men who say they have dishonored them in some way, such as rejecting a marriage proposal. Even children have been scarred. A man may get revenge on an enemy by burning the faces of his wife and daughters, and disfigured victims seldom have the means to seek surgical help. The crime is most common in Bangladesh and Afghanistan, but also occurs in Pakistan and India and other parts of the world. Women are increasingly being attacked by husbands for minor offences, such as not having dinner ready or refusing sex. The perpetrators are seldom prosecuted.

Bhutan: According to a 2011 study by the National Statistics Bureau, almost a quarter of female respondents admitted domestic abuse. Seventy percent of women in the study believed that wife beating is acceptable.

Afghanistan: Afghan President Hamid Karzai issued a decree in 2009 banning violence against women. Yet over 87% of women in this country are victims of domestic mistreatment, according to UN estimates. And a 2011 Thomson Reuters Foundation survey named Afghanistan the most dangerous country in the world for women.

Egypt: An article in the Egyptian criminal code says that if a woman has been beaten by her husband "with good intentions," no punitive damages can be obtained.

Lebanon: A parliamentary committee presented with the draft of a new law to prevent violence against women in 2012, removed marital rape as well as psychological and economic violence. One committee member declared that marital rape did not exist, even though there are hundreds of reported cases each year.

Saudi Arabia: Rape and domestic violence are widespread problems, and women have no redress.

Turkey: A 2011 study found that 42% of this country's females experience sexual and physical abuse at some point.

United Arab Emirates: The penal code gives men the legal right to discipline their wives and children, and the Federal Supreme Court has upheld a husband's right to "chastise" his wife and children with physical abuse.

Yemen: There are currently no laws on the books against marital rape.

Pakistan: The senate passed a Domestic Violence Bill in 2012 that makes violence against women or children an offence. Previously, a man who beat his wife or children couldn't be arrested because it was considered a domestic affair. If enforced, this bill will be a great step forward. However, police indifference is an ongoing obstacle.

The Human Rights Commission of Pakistan states that *"a rape occurs every two hours, and a gang rape every eight hours. One in every 12,500 women suffers rape."* So do a large number of children each year, almost all of them Christians or Hindus, members of minority religions, according to the Society for the Protection of the Rights of the Child.

- Under Pakistan's Hudood Ordinance of 1979 which governs punishment for adultery and rape, statutory rape (previously defined as sex with or without the consent of a girl under the age of 14) was no longer a crime. In addition, the legal possibility of marital rape was eliminated. The latter still stands, although a Women's Protection Bill was passed to amend the Hudood Ordinance in 2006. The bill allows judges to try rape cases under civil law rather than Sharia (Islamic) law, doing away with the requirement of four witnesses.

The great majority of police, doctors and prosecutors in Pakistan tend not only to disbelieve but to belittle women who report a rape. Police have been known to threaten and intimidate victims, and accept bribes from accused males.

One attorney openly declared, *"I don't believe in rape cases. Women's consent is always there. If rape exists, it happens in only one % of cases."* In fact, the woman who files a case against a man is herself in danger of prosecution, unless she can prove that she was not a willing partner in adultery or fornication. In other words, the victim herself is guilty until proven innocent. Human rights workers say that approximately half the women who report a rape are charged with adultery without any substantiating evidence, and languish in jail. Even when acquitted such women may fall victim to "honor killings" by male members of their family, who consider their honor compromised. In traditional villages, *girls or women who bear an illegitimate child after being molested may be stoned to death.*

Pakistan has no specific legislation against domestic violence. Abuse in the home is most likely to be dismissed as a family matter. In the rare case that it does go to a criminal court, a monetary settlement (blood money) or retribution may be awarded.

- Percentage of women aged 15 to 49 who think that a husband/partner is justified in hitting or beating his wife/partner under certain circumstances:[10] Afghanistan and Jordan, 90%; Mali, 87%; Guinea and Timo-Leste, 86%; Laos, 81%; Central African Republic, 80%; South Sudan, 79%; Somalia and Democratic Republic of the Congo, 76%; Gambia, 75%; Tajikistan, 74%; Sierra Leone and Burundi, 73%; Niger, Tuvalu and Uzbekistan, 70%; Algeria and Bhutan, 68%.

Action Step:
November 25th has been designated by the UN as the International Day for the Elimination of Violence against Women. Explore the resources available from some of the websites listed in Appendix 2 of this book, and support the agencies that work to defeat gender violence.

*See also section called "Vital Statistics: Honor Killings"

(Endnotes)
1   http://www.wlv.ac.uk/default.aspx?page=33020
2   http://www.telegraph.co.uk/news/religion/9976822/Sharia-courts-putting-women-at-risk-CPS-warns.html
3   http://csis.org/publication/latin-america-women-still-confront-violence
4   Ibid.
5   Ibid.
6   http://saynotoviolence.org/issue/facts-and-figures
7   http://www.infochangeindia.org/women/news/one-rape-every-half-hour-in-india-a-dowry-death-every-75-minutes.html;   http://www.indianchild.com/girlchild/rights-of-girl-child.htm
8   http://in.reuters.com/article/2013/06/14/india-rape-women-2012-report-idINDEE95D0B920130614
9   http://globalvoicesonline.org/2013/02/22/bangladesh-raises-voice-to-end-violence-against-women/
10 http://www.childinfo.org/attitudes_data.php

SOS: Education

Two-thirds of the world's 774 million illiterates are women. Of the 72 million children who are growing up without an education, 34 million are girls. Less than a third of all girls are enrolled in secondary school.[1]

MAJOR FACTORS OF ILLITERACY

Poverty: Families that are just managing to survive are unlikely to make schooling a priority. Disabled, displaced, migrant children and minors living in conflict or post-disaster areas are also greatly disadvantaged. Situations of destitution usually lead to child labor and, for girls, early marriages.

Multiple languages: Most of the world's illiterate people live in nations in which scores or even hundreds of languages are spoken. Some minority, indigenous languages or dialects have no written alphabet or very little in print.

Gender discrimination: Especially in patriarchal societies, this is still very much part of the equation. In Arab States, Central Asia and Southern and Western Asia, privileged treatment is traditionally given to males. Girls are destined to marry or work in the family home, whereas boys are entitled to receive an education.[2] Sons are considered a "long term investment" since they are expected to care for aging parents.

The world is a long way from achieving the United Nation's 2015 international development goal of universal primary education for boys and girls alike.

Female School Life Expectancy*

Countries where girls average the fewest years of schooling:

Somalia (2 years), Eritrea (4); Central African Republic, Chad, Cote d'Ivoire, Djibouti, Niger (5)

Countries where girls average the most years of schooling:

Australia (21 years), Iceland and New Zealand (20), Cuba (19), and Denmark, Finland, Ireland, Norway, Slovenia (18)

*Source: World Fact Book, 2013

Female Literacy Rates*

Countries with the lowest rates:

Afghanistan (12.6%), Niger (15.1%), Burkina Faso (15.2%), South Sudan (16%)

Countries with the highest rates:

Andorra, Finland, Greenland, Lichtenstein, Luxembourg (100%)

Azerbaijan, Barbados, Lithuania (99.7%)

Armenia (99.4%)

Belgium, Bermuda, Iceland, Ireland, Japan, North Korea, Monaco, Netherlands, New Zealand, United States (99%)

*Source: World Fact Book, 2013

ASIA: *Only about half of women* aged 15 and over can read and write. A third of Indian girls do not finish primary school. Most families still don't allow a woman to work, except in female-dominated fields like teaching and health care. But urban and middle class mothers are increasingly aware that their daughters will have a better chance in the workplace through education.

Pakistan

In the federally administered tribal areas of Pakistan's North West Frontier, female illiteracy is 96 percent—much higher than in other parts of the country. The Taliban destroyed hundreds of schools and threatened displaced families with violence if they sent their girls to school.[3] A 14-year-old Pakistani girl in the Swat Valley made world headlines in 2012 when she was shot in the head for defying the Taliban, determined to have an education. Malala Yousafzai was airlifted to Britain where skull surgery saved her life and where she has remained to attend school. In 2013, Shahnaz Nazli, a 41-year-old teacher on her way with her child to work at an all girls' school, was shot dead. The Pakistani government has now agreed for the first time to legislate compulsory free education and provide stipends for three million children.

Afghanistan: Just six percent of women 25 and older have received any formal education. The Taliban are again growing in influence, and attacks by armed groups opposed to educating females continue to make schooling difficult. Some girls have been maimed by acid attacks or had their drinking water poisoned.[4]

Turkey's president approved a controversial bill in 2012 that extended compulsory education to 12 years, but allowed home schooling after the first eight, which critics said could encourage the practice of child brides.

AFRICA: Of the world's 22 countries where over half the population is illiterate, 15 are in Africa. In 47 out of 54 countries, girls have less than a 50 percent chance of completing primary school. In **sub-Saharan Africa,** the gender gap widens significantly at the secondary level, where around six girls are enrolled for every ten boys. [UNESCO] Secondary school completion rates for adolescent girls is below five percent in nineteen countries.

Somalia: Only 42 percent of primary school age children are in school, and of these, only 36 percent are girls. 28 percent of girls are in secondary school. Just 15 percent of the teaching force are women, with the majority of them unqualified. [UNICEF]

Uganda: 85 percent of girls leave school early. [GirlEffect]

MIDDLE EAST: School enrollment for girls in **Yemen** is the lowest of all Middle Eastern countries, with only about half of girls attending primary school. Education is not given as high a priority as chastity; mixed gender schools and the shortage of female teachers means that girls are often kept at home, especially in rural areas. Early marriages are traditional.

In **Saudi Arabia,** only 23% of girls were enrolled in a secondary school back in 1980. Now, however, the percentage of girls having higher education has greatly increased and the government provides many scholarship programs. Women's university test scores in Saudi Arabia routinely outstrip men's. They are still forbidden to take some subjects such as journalism, architecture and engineering, however; and they cannot practice law. 85 percent are employed in education.

LATIN AMERICA has fared better overall in educating girls but there are still major gaps. For instance, under a third of women in Bolivia can read and write, according to UNESCO. Indigenous people groups within countries are often largely ignored. And the prevalence of migrant and child labor in mining, farming and banana plantations in some areas also contributes to uneven school attendance for both boys and girls. Regarding higher education, women in the male-oriented cultures of Latin America and the Caribbean have been discouraged from entering engineering or hard science fields, with the exception of medicine. Although girls perform better in schools than boys and more continue to high levels of education, males still earn far more in the workplace and violence against women remains high.

NORTH AMERICA: In the **USA**, a surprising one in four girls do not finish high school. The dropout rate is even higher for girls from minorities. [National Women's Law Center] Twenty percent of adultAmericans are functional illiterates. Girls in **Canada** show more commitment to their education than boys and are less likely to drop out. However, 42% of Canadian adults between the ages of 16 and 65 have low literacy skills.[5]

EUROPE'S "functional illiterates": One in five 15 year olds, as well as nearly 75 million European adults, lack basic reading and writing skills according to an EU report.[6] A World Literacy Foundation report in 2012 adds that 47% of Italy's adults struggle to read and write; so do one in five adults in Ireland and the UK, 18% of residents in Belgium, 16% in Switzerland, 14% in Germany and 11% in the Netherlands. This means they may have trouble filling out a job application, reading a bank statement or labels on food products.[7]

Europe has a **Roma** (gypsy) population of 10 to 12 million. Education levels are particularly low among these people, worldwide. UNESCO states that half of Roma children fail to complete a primary education. Girls are often married extremely young, depriving them of educational opportunities.

How Education Affects Population Growth, Infant Mortality Rates and Income

- Literate women average two children per family while illiterate women commonly have six to eight children.

- The health of a mother and her children have a direct correlation to education. Besides having fewer children, educated women are more likely to use health clinics and return to them if there is no improvement. In fact, education is one of the main factors influencing mortality rates of children under five. A child born to a woman who can read is 50 percent more likely to survive past the age of five. For every year of schooling a mother has received, the likelihood that her child dies as an infant declines by 10 percent.

- A recent study of 63 countries also showed that improvements in education for women was "the single largest contributor" to *declines in malnutrition* among children.

- The families of women with some education tend to have better housing, clothing, income, water and sanitation. As literacy rates double, so does the average per capita income.[8]

- About **75 percent** of children out of primary school in developing countries have mothers who did not go to school. [UNICEF]

Nearly a billion people entered the 21st century unable to read a book, or sign their own names.

Action Steps:

The UN established the "International Day of the Girl" on October 11, 2012, to highlight the fact that child marriages prevent girls from finishing their education and fulfilling their potential. Promote the 10x10 Campaign, a global initiative that advocates for the improvement of girls' education around the world. Also support Plan-UK's "Because I am a Girl" campaign and other initiatives that can be found in Appendix 2 under "Education."

See the related section of this book titled "Vital Statistics: Child Marriages".

(Endnotes)
1 http://dayofthegirl.org/girls-issues/
2 http://childrensrightsportal.org/world/right-to-education/
3 http://www.brookings.edu/research/opinions/2009/06/11-pakistan-education-winthrop
4 http://www.cnn.com/2012/09/26/world/asia/cnnheroes-afghan-schoolgirls
5 http://www.literacy.ca/literacy/literacy-sub/
6 http://ec.europa.eu/education/literacy/what-eu/high-level-group/documents/literacy-report.pdf
7 http://www.thesun.co.uk/sol/homepage/news/politics/4226467/Illiterate-Britain Scandal-of-one-in-5-adults-battling-to-read-and-write.html
8 http://www-01.sil.org/literacy/wom_lit.htm

SOS: Female Genital Mutilation

About 140 million girls and women worldwide are living with the consequences of genital mutilation, according to the World Health Organization. Another 6,000 girls every day are at risk.

The practice of female genital cutting or mutilation (FGM) is sometimes referred to as female circumcision, but this term is anatomically incorrect and applies only to a rare procedure. It also creates a false analogy to male circumcision, a practice which, unlike FGM, has religious significance and proven health benefits.

Even though FGM has no foundation in Islamic scripture or law, one in five Muslim girls today live in a community that sanctions some form of the practice. Few religious leaders have spoken up against it.

The highest prevalence rates are in Africa, where it is practiced in 29 countries even though it is illegal in some of them. More than half of all the women and girls in some countries have undergone excision. These numbers are not decreasing.

▶ *What exactly is FGM?*

Female genital mutilation refers to the removal of part or all of the female genitalia. There are three types, the most severe being infibulation which is carried out upon an estimated 15% of girls that undergo FGM. This procedure consists of clitoridectomy (removing all or part of the clitoris) and excision (removing all or part of the *labia minora,* the inner "lips" that surround the vagina; and cutting of the *labia majora* or outer "lips") to create raw surfaces. These are then stitched or held together in order to form a cover over the vagina when they heal. A small hole is left to allow urine and menstrual blood to escape. Some less conventional forms of infibulation remove less tissue and leave a larger opening. The vast majority (85%) of FGM in Africa consists of either clitoridectomy or excision. This is also practiced in the Middle East: Egypt, Oman, Yemen and the United Arab Emirates. In Djibouti and the Central African Republic, an estimated 95% of women are infibulated.

Cutting may be carried out on a girl any time from soon after birth to during her first pregnancy. Sometimes it is regarded as a coming-of-age ritual. But the most common age is between four and eight years old. The person who performs it can be an older woman or barber, a midwife or traditional healer or a qualified doctor.

Only the wealthy have access to doctors and anesthetics. The vast majority of girls are given no preparation or painkiller. They are simply held down while the appointed "surgeon" proceeds with a broken glass, tin lid, scissors, razor blade or other cutting instrument. When infibulation takes place, thorns or stitches may be used to hold the two sides of the *labia majora* together, and the girl's legs may be bound together for up to 40 days. Antiseptic powder is sometimes applied, or, more usually, pastes containing herbs, milk, eggs, ashes or dung, which are believed to facilitate healing. The girl may be taken to a specially designated place to recover where, if the mutilation has been carried out as part of an initiation ceremony, she receives traditional teaching.

▶ *WHY* FGM?

In most societies where female circumcision is practiced it is a deeply rooted part of the culture. Girls who go through it are considered cleaner and more feminine. Since they will not be accepted into womanhood—and certainly not marriage—without this ritual, the pressure to conform is enormous. Parents also believe that FGM reduces a girl's sexual desire and so protects the chastity of their daughters—although many mistakenly believe it actually increases fertility! Infibulation, in particular, is seen to safeguard the family honor.

Mauritanian women scored a victory in 2012 when Muslim clerics and scholars declared a *fatwa*, or religious decree, against the centuries-old practice. About 72 percent of the women in Mauritania have undergone FGM.

Figures suggest that up to 90% of Egyptian females suffer mutilation. FGM was legally banned in 2008 but it is still commonplace, and some politicians continue to call for a legal revival of the practice.

> *"How can we leave our daughters uncircumcised?"* **a mayor of one Egyptian city was quoted.** *"The government can do what it wants and we, too, will do what we want. We will all circumcise our daughters, no matter what the punishments."*

A 43-year-old female biology professor from Sudan explained,"*We are brought up to believe that all sorts of evil things will happen to us if we are not circumcised. It is done at such a young age....It doesn't really sink in, what has been done, and the problems later when you are a woman, seem to have no connection to it.*"

▶THE CONSEQUENCES

There are no health benefits to FGM. The immediate effects can include extreme pain, shock, bleeding, tetanus or bacterial infection, urine retention, open sores—even death. Girls who go through it are often scarred for life, both mentally and physically. In the days following the procedure, serious infections and abscesses often develop. Infibulation may also result in long-term urinary tract infections, kidney damage, stones, cysts, infections from obstruction of the menstrual flow, even infertility.

A possible additional danger from all types of female genital mutilation is that repeated use of the same instrument on several girls, as is sometimes the case, can cause the spread of HIV. Lasting damage to the genital area can also increase the risk of HIV transmission during intercourse.

Many women report that on their wedding nights, their husbands had to use a knife to cut a wider opening for intercourse. As one can imagine, impromptu surgery like this can cause even further damage to young brides.

During childbirth, scar tissue left from genital cutting may tear. Women who have been infibulated must be cut to allow delivery. After each birth the opening is re-stitched. [1]

▶IMMIGRANT COMMUNITIES WORLDWIDE

Immigrants and refugees have carried female cutting practices to countries in the developed world. In spite of a legal ban in most of the West, a half million girls are still forced to undergo this cruel and unnecessary procedure in Europe: as many as 75,000 women in Britain, 65,000 in France, 30,000 in Germany.[1] Thousands more suffer in silence in Australia and the USA. To avoid prosecution, parents often take their girls back to their country of origin for the ritual.

"I have nightmares. I have never coped.... I need surgery. I have scar tissues.... I will live with this for the rest of my life....But one thing for sure, I will never stop voicing out against FGM. I am living to tell and be a voice for the voiceless." –Mashua, a victim in Kenya

A number of groups are campaigning against this widespread violation of human rights. (See agencies listed in Appendix 2.) In some places, however, there are increasing reports of attacks and death threats upon girls and women who speak out against female genital cutting.

In 2008, the World Health Assembly passed a resolution on the elimination of female genital mutilation and in December 2012, the UN General Assembly accepted a similar resolution. Nations still have a long way to go in making this legislation a reality.

Action Step

"FGM" in Appendix 2 lists a number of worldwide initiatives aimed at stopping this crippling practice. All of us need to get behind their efforts and encourage others to get on board.

"Hear my prayer, LORD, listen to my cry for help; do not be deaf to my weeping. I dwell with you as an alien, a stranger, as all my fathers were." Psalm 39:12

(Endnotes)

[1] http://www.desertflowerfoundation.org/en/what-is-fgm/fgm-in-europe-facts/

SOS: Female Infanticide and Feticide

The deliberate killing of female children, before and after birth, has been called "the biggest single holocaust in human history."

The death toll from gendercide throughout the centuries would amount to mega-millions. Baby girls have been murdered because of a preference for boys since the days of ancient Rome. Today female feticide is most often found in South, Southeast and Central Asia.

INDIA

> Some three million Indian girls were "missing" from this country's population in 2011 due to female infanticide, according to *Children in India 2012: A Statistical Appraisal.* The preference for sons has resulted in 12 million girls being aborted over the past three decades. *[Lancet]*

▶The birth of a girl is often bad news to a poor Indian family because of the enormous dowry that will eventually be required of them when she is married. Even though the custom of payment to a bridegroom's family was officially prohibited by the Dowry Act of 1961, the system is still very much alive. A dowry can cost several times what the head of the house earns in a year, and bankrupt the family. A son, on the other hand, will carry on the family name and also attract a dowry that will bring prosperity. Parents may therefore choose to terminate a girl's life before it even begins. The development of prenatal sex determination tests in the 1970's led to large-scale, sex-selective abortions. Even upper caste families may see feticide as an option. Sex-selective abortion has been illegal for twenty years, but comparatively few doctors have been prosecuted. India has over 40,000 registered ultrasound clinics and many more that are unregistered. Their advertisements urge the investment of a few hundred rupees on a gender test in order to save thousands on a future dowry.

▶Pregnant women who cannot afford prenatal tests are obliged to wait until they give birth to determine their babies' sex. Girl children may then be smothered, strangled or simply allowed to starve to death. Other infants have been fed salt, milk laced with poison or dry, unhulled rice that punctured their windpipes. More modern methods are now usually employed to avoid detection, like inducing severe diarrhea with a few drops of alcohol, or wrapping the newborn in a wet towel to cause pneumonia.

▶Entire villages exist in Rajasthan, northern India, where the birth of daughters has not been allowed for years. "Girls are buried in the desert and no one in the clan ever inquires about the newborn or mourns the loss," confirmed a senior police officer. The resulting unbalanced sex ratio has given rise to wife-sharing in Rajasthan and other states.

▶ *Only a handful of mothers in recent years have received life imprisonment sentences for infanticide;* a few others are serving six months to three years. However, the decision is usually made by the woman's husband or in-laws; she is as much a victim as her child and is given no choice but to obey or suffer the consequences.

▶ The huge number of feticides and infanticides in India means the ratio of females to males continues to decline. The 2012 average is 940 girls to 1000 boys. The Indian child rights organization CRY estimates say that about 12 million girls are born in India every year; however, one million of these girls die by the age of one.

PAKISTAN

▶ The murder of infants by poverty-stricken parents is also on the rise in Pakistan. According to a spokesperson for the charitable Edhi Foundation, more and more bodies of infants are being collected from the streets. "I would say there has been a 100 per cent increase over the past decade in the number of bodies of infants we find. Nine out of 10 are girls." He added that of 1,210 bodies were found in 2010.[1]

NORTH KOREA

A number of reports from North Korean defectors point to the likelihood that forced abortion and infanticide are common practices in North Korean detention camps.

CHINA

China leads the world in gendercide. In 2013 the Chinese Health Ministry announced that 336 million abortions have been performed in the last four decades. A great proportion of babies that die through abortion and institutionalized killing and neglect are girls.

Infanticide of girl babies in China goes back far before pre-People's Republic days. Until the turn of the century, daughters were often given no name at all. Today those born in rural areas may still be given the names "Alidi," "Zhaodi," or "Yindi"—all of which mean *"Bring a Little Brother."* Daughters have also been called "maggots in the rice" because they take food that could go to nourish boys. In the Chinese culture, the male can earn more and it is the son who looks after parents in old age. Although female infanticide largely disappeared during the 1950's through 1970's, it surged back in the 1980's after the government imposed a "one child" policy. The policy also led to forced abortions and forced sterilizations. A woman who has an illegal child can be fined a "social burden compensation fee" of over $27,000. The government has officially outlawed the use of ultrasound for sex determination, but many doctors still use it.

In 2013 campaigns were launched in several Chinese provinces, requiring all women of childbearing age to be fitted with IUDs or else, if they already have two children, undergo tubal ligation or sterilization. Those who comply within a certain time are given financial rewards; those who don't will be barred from social security and hospital services and their children cannot enroll in school.[2]

120 boys are born for every 100 girls, the worst gender ratio in the world. It is predicted that there will be 30 million more Chinese men than women of marriageable age by 2020. Leaders fear this situation is damaging the country's social and economic stability, and further encouraging the trade in kidnapped women.

IN THE WEST

Sex-selective abortions are not limited to Asian countries. This is in fact a growing trend in the West. In **Sweden**, for example, the abortion of babies on the basis of their sex is not illegal. In **Britain**, MPs in 2013 called on the government to compile statistics on the gender of aborted babies after it was found that women in "certain communities" were giving birth to an usually higher number of males than females.[3]

Six studies in the past four years indicate that there are thousands of "missing girls" in the **U.S.** as well, many because of sex-selective abortions, especially among immigrants from developing nations. Only three states ban the practice. The Prenatal Non-Discrimination Act, which would have banned such abortions nationally, was defeated in 2012.

Canada is the only western nation with no protection for the unborn. Since 1969 over four million children have been aborted; this year another 100,000 babies will be put to death at taxpayer expense. Abnormal gender ratios in communities with a large proportion of Indians, together with the growth of sex-determination testing, also point to the existence of sex-selective abortions.[4]

Action Steps

* *The 11th of October was established by the United Nations as the International Day of the Girl, to advance the lives of girls across the globe. Learn more at dayofthegirl.org and bring this effort to the attention of people you know.*

* *Support campaigns like those of the Society for the Protection of Unborn Children, Women's Rights Without Frontiers and The 50 Million Missing Campaign. Internet addresses are listed in Appendix 2 under "Female Infanticide."*

"For you created my inmost being; you knit me together in my mother's womb....Your eyes saw my unformed body. All the days ordained for me were written in your book before one of them came to be." —Psalm 139:13-16

(Endnotes)

1 http://tribune.com.pk/story/105019/infanticide-on-the-rise-in-pakistan-statistics/

2 http://www.christiannewswire.com/news/6515972254.html

3 http://www.christianconcern.com/our-concerns/abortion/mps-urge-government-to-monitor-gender-of-aborted-babies

4 http://www.nationalreviewofmedicine.com/issue/2007/09_15/4_policy_politics02_15.html#top

SOS: Gender Inequalities

Statistics make it clear that in no region of the world are women and men equal in legal, social or economic rights.

These pages touch upon disparities between men and women in areas besides health and education, which are covered in other sections.

GENDER INEQUALITY INDEX

The United Nation's Human Development Reports include a Gender Inequality Index, which measures nations for inequality between males and females in the areas of reproductive health, empowerment and participation in the labor market. The most recent survey finds the country with the greatest gender gaps is **Yemen**, followed by **Afghanistan, Niger, Saudi Arabia, the Democratic Republic of the Congo, Liberia, the Central African Republic and Mali.**

POLITICAL PARTICIPATION

Women continue to be under-represented in most countries worldwide. An average of about one in five members of national parliaments are women as of this printing, with Arab states having the lowest numbers followed by those in the Pacific area. Women in Nordic countries have the highest representation. Women ministers are much more likely to be elected or appointed to serve in social rather than executive, political, economic or legal departments of government.

Disparity is most obvious when looking at the number of women candidates running for local or national office. In **Armenia**, for instance, only nine women were elected to a total of 397 posts as mayor or local government chief in 2012. In **Kenya's** 2013 general elections, several female candidates withdrew from the race after male rivals used physical and psychological violence to intimidate them. Women in **Pakistan** had to defy Taliban death threats to run in 2013 general elections, even though the chance of winning was slim. A constitutional body in **Iran** has ruled that women cannot run in presidential elections.

In 2013, out of 189 governments, women held only 17 of the highest positions of state. Against the odds and in spite of the machismo culture, women in **Latin America** are moving up on the political ladder with more female heads of state than any other area.

WAGES and EMPLOYMENT OPPORTUNITIES

*"Women make up two-thirds of the world's work force, yet earn one-tenth of the world's income and hold only one percent of total assets." —*Barber B. Conable Jr., former president of World Bank

* Women's nominal wages are an average 17 percent lower than men's. [UNIFEM]

* There is a direct link between increased female labor participation and economic growth. It is estimated that if women's paid employment rates were raised to the same level as men's, America's GDP would be nine percent higher; the Euro-zone's would be 13 percent higher, and Japan's would be boosted by 16 percent. [ESCAP]

* In **Arab states**, only 28 percent of women participate in the workforce. [WORLD BANK]

* In the **USA**, a study of California's 400 largest companies showed that men still hold roughly nine of every 10 highest-paid management and board positions.[1] In 2012, the ratio of women's to men's median weekly full-time earnings was 80.9 percent, a decline of more than one percentage point since 2011 when the ratio was 82.2 percent. This corresponds to a weekly gender wage gap of 19.1 percent for 2012. Women's median weekly earnings in 2012 were $691, a marginal decline compared to 2011; men's median weekly earnings were $854, a marginal increase compared to 2011. [Institute for Women's Policy Research, Fact Sheet]

* **Latin America and the Caribbean:** Women with more education than men are still concentrated in lower-paid occupations such as teaching, health care or the service sector. The wage gap has been decreasing in recent years, but at a pace that remains slow. In **Mexico**, women in paid employment devote an additional 33 hours to domestic chores per week, while men's average weekly contribution is six hours. [UNDP][2]

* Women constitute around 60 to 80 percent of the export manufacturing workforce in the developing world, but the global economic crisis is expected to plunge 22 million females into unemployment. When there are cutbacks, women are the first to be fired. [ILO]

INEQUALITIES UNDER ISLAM

As the UN's Gender Inequality Index (above) indicates, most of the worst gender gaps occur in Islamic countries. A new report on gender-based violence written by the U.S. Hudson Institute for the World Watch List describes how a profound lack of equality between men and women in Muslim countries means that all women in these societies are structurally vulnerable to systematic violence and discrimination in their daily lives.[3]

Adultery and Other Moral Issues

- **Iranian** law reads: "*The stoning of an adulterer or adulteress will be carried on while each is placed in a hole and covered with soil—he up to his waist, and she up to the line above her breast.*" Under Islamic law, if you can escape and run away you are allowed to go free. Obviously no woman can escape if she is buried almost to her neck!

- Under **Libya's** Qaddafi, girls and women who survived sexual assaults or were suspected of moral crimes were dumped into "social rehabilitation centers." These were effectively prisons from which they could not leave unless a man agreed to marry them or their families took them back.

- The law in the **United Arab Emirates** (UAE) provides little redress for rape victims. Over 50 percent of women residents in the UAE who responded to a survey said they would not report a rape to police because it was the victim who was punished or threatened for having premarital sex. The assault itself would not be properly investigated.

- In **Kuwait**, both married men and married women who commit adultery are punished by one to two years of imprisonment. However, men face this penalty only when they act with the knowledge that the woman is married, whereas women are punished even if they act without such knowledge.

- 600 women and girls in **Afghanistan** were imprisoned for "moral crimes" in 2013, a 50 percent rise over the previous year and a half. These "moral crimes" usually involve flight from unlawful forced and underage marriages below 16 or domestic violence including beatings, stabbings, burnings, rapes, forced prostitution, kidnapping, and threats of "honor killing." Virtually none of the cases had led even to an investigation of the abuse, let alone prosecution or punishment. "Running away," or fleeing home without permission, is not a crime under the Afghan criminal code, but the Afghan Supreme Court has instructed its judges to treat women and girls who flee as criminals.[4]

- Amnesty International and Somali media reported in 2012 that Islamic militia in **Somalia** accused a 13-year-old girl of adultery after she told officials three men had raped her. She was stoned to death by dozens of men in a stadium filled with 1,000 people.[5]

Custody Rights

- In **Bahrain**, where family law is not codified, judges have complete power to deny women custody of their children for the most arbitrary reasons. Bahraini women who have been courageous enough to expose and challenge these violations in 2003 were sued for slander by 11 family court judges.[6]

- In **Yemen**, custody of children is highly biased towards husbands, as men are considered the natural guardians of children, while women are viewed as physical custodians but have no legal rights.

Divorce

- **Iran's** Civil Code, Article 1133, states, "A man can divorce his wife whenever he so chooses and does not have to give her advance notice."

- In **Lebanon**, a battered woman cannot file for divorce on the basis of abuse without the testimony of an eyewitness. A doctor's certificate verifying abuse is not enough.[7]

Heaven & Hell

- *"Whereas out of every thousand men only one will go to hell. Yet, out of every thousand women only one will be found in heaven."*

- Mohammed said, *"I was shown the Hellfire and that the majority of its dwellers are women."*

The statements above are *hadiths*, part of the traditions rather than the Qur'an itself, but highly respected as what the Prophet is reputed to have said or done or permitted. In all writings, the delights of paradise are mostly promised to faithful men. As a result many Muslim women live in fear of death.

Inheritance

- *"To the male a portion equal to that of two females."* This quote from the Qur'an, Surah 4:11, indicates that a daughter should receive only half the inheritance of her brother. When a woman's husband dies she receives only a quarter of the legacy. If there are several wives they must divide the quarter portion. In the **United Arab Emirates,** females can only inherit one-third of assets while men are entitled to two-thirds.

Prayer & Fasting

- **Iranian** girls of nine years are expected to wear *hijab* (Islamic dress), rise for dawn prayers and go without food and drink from dawn to dusk during the month of Ramadan. Boys are not required to take part in the fast until they are fifteen.

Travel

- Husbands in **Egypt** and **Bahrain** can file an official complaint at the airport to forbid their wives from leaving the country for any reason. In **Iraq, Libya, Jordan, Morocco, Oman and Yemen**, married women must have their husband's written permission to travel abroad, and they may be prevented from doing so for any reason. In **Saudi Arabia**, women must obtain written permission from their closest male relative to leave the country or travel on public transportation between different parts of the kingdom.[8] Nor are Saudi women permitted driver's licenses.

The Veil & Clothing Restrictions

The Qur'an does not require women to be completely veiled or secluded. Each Muslim culture imposes its own dress code for females, ranging from a simple headscarf to an all-enveloping head-to-toe cloak or *burqa*, like those worn in Afghanistan and Yemen. The most conservative women also wear gloves. Interestingly, little attention is given to modesty for men, although the Prophet Muhammed instructed that they should cover themselves "from navel to knee." Among North Africa's Tuareg people it is the male, not female, who veils his face to prevent the enemy from knowing what he's thinking. Women, say these men, have nothing to hide! Most Muslims disregard the customs of this people group, however, since in Arabic, "tuareg" means "the abandoned of God."

- Women in **Saudi Arabia** can suffer corporal punishment from religious police if they are not completely covered. Rules for female attire are so stringent that in 2002, religious police stopped schoolgirls from fleeing their burning school building because they weren't wearing the proper headscarves and robes. One witness said he saw three policemen beating students who tried to leave. 15 girls died in the blaze.[9]

- A number of cases have been reported of acid thrown in the faces of unveiled women by extremists in parts of **Pakistan** and **Afghanistan**. Coptic girls on **Egyptian** trains and buses have been attacked with scissors by hijab-wearing Muslim women who cut off the girls' hair because they weren't wearing headscarves. While many Muslim women would defend veiling, others deplore being forced to cover themselves.

- Article 102 of **Iran's** Constitution reads: "Women who appear on streets and in public without the prescribed 'Islamic Hijab' will be condemned to 74 strokes of the lash."

Voting Rights

- **Kuwaiti** women were finally granted full voting rights in 2005, for the first time in the country's history.

- The **United Arab Emirates** allowed the first vote for both men and women in 2006.

- After postponing women's suffrage in 2009 and again in 2011, King Abdullah announced in 2013 that women in **Saudi Arabia** would be allowed to vote, and will be allowed to stand as candidates in municipal elections in 2015.

- Some 10 million **Pakistani** women are simply unregistered to vote, largely because they have not been granted identity cards.

Witness

In most Sharia (Islamic) courts of law, a woman's testimony has only half the worth of a man's; therefore two women witnesses are required in contrast to just one male. Also, the testimony of a Christian is worth half that of a Muslim.

Other Rights

Kuwaiti women remain prohibited from serving as judges and joining the military, they have unequal marital rights, and they are not allowed to pass their nationality on to their children and foreign-born husbands.

They also lack equal rights in laws regulating social security, pensions and inheritance.

"Yet the Lord longs to be gracious to you; he rises to show you compassion. For the Lord is a God of justice. Blessed are all who wait for him!" Isaiah 30:18

(Endnotes)

1   http://gsm.ucdavis.edu/innovator-article/glass-ceiling
2   http://www.iadb.org/en/news/webstories/2012-10-15/wage-gap-between-men-and-women,10155.html
3   http://www.worldwatchmonitor.org/research/2533678
4   http://www.hrw.org/news/2013/05/21/afghanistan-surge-women-jailed-moral-crimes
5   http://www.huffingtonpost.com/2008/11/02/13yearold-rape-victim-sto_n_140242.html
6   http://forums.canadiancontent.net/international-politics/61857-womens-rights-middle-east.html
7   Ibid.
8   Ibid.
9   http://news.bbc.co.uk/1/hi/1874471.stm

SOS: Girl Soldiers

▶ *Tens of thousands of girls* number among the estimated 300,000 children fighting in worldwide armed conflicts at any one time. Some of them carry a fully-automatic assault weapon by the age of seven or eight.

Children are sometimes called the "invisible soldiers" because governments deny they exist. They are kept out of media attention and often end up vanishing: either killed, maimed or abandoned. The vast majority of child soldiers are in the ranks of non-governmental or rebel armed groups.

> One 14-year-old girl abducted to serve a rebel group in Sierra Leone said, *"I've seen people get their hands cut off, a ten-year-old girl raped and then die, and so many men and women burned alive . . . So many times I just cried inside my heart because I didn't dare cry out loud."*[1]

Why girls?

Both boys and girls are used for cooking, fetching water and washing clothes for an army. They also carry supplies and equipment and can be used as human shields. But an average of 40% of child soldiers are girls. These adolescents are routinely raped and may be handed over to rebel fighters as wives or sex slaves.

Increasing numbers of girls go into actual combat. Cambodia's Khmer Rouge put them at the front to take the worst of the fighting. Or girls are sent into enemy territory to act as human mine detectors, or spies.

Susan, a 16-year-old Ugandan abductee, told of her experience: "One boy tried to escape, but he was caught... His hands were tied, and then they made us, the other new captives, kill him with a stick. I felt sick. I knew this boy from before. We were from the same village. I refused to kill him and they told me they would shoot me. They pointed a gun at me, so I had to do it. The boy was asking me, 'Why are you doing this?' I said I had no choice. After we killed him, they made us smear his blood on our arms.... They said we had to do this so we would not fear death and so we would not try to escape....I still dream about the boy from my village who I killed. I see him in my dreams, and he is talking to me and saying I killed him for nothing, and I am crying." [2]

How are girls recruited?

Some governments make it compulsory for under-18's to serve in their military forces. These include countries that signed the UN's Optional Protocol against this practice in 2002 (see reference below). A large number of other countries, including Australia and Canada, accept 17-year-old volunteers. Boys in Bolivia can be conscripted as young as 14, and a large portion of this country's armed forces are under 18. Child soldiers have long been recruited by Yemeni militia and Iraq's al Quaeda wing—sometimes called the "Youth of Heaven." The UN also names Somalia's Al-Shabaab extremists as abductors of children for use in fighting. Children in some places have been shot for trying to escape recruitment.[3]

- *Rebel groups abduct many thousands* from their homes or right off the street, or press-gang them. Myanmar (Burma) is the only country in Asia where government armed forces forcibly recruit and use children 12 to 18. Whole groups of schoolchildren have been surrounded and conscripted.[4]

- *Destitute parents may give or sell their daughters* to armed groups. According to a study in Sierra Leone, "many mothers have remarked on the joy of seeing their 10-year-old dressed in brand new military attire, carrying an AK-47. For some families the looted property that child soldiers brought home further convinced them of the need to send more children to the war front to augment scarce income."

- *A significant number of girls volunteer.* They may be idealistically motivated, or they may want to get revenge for violence done to their families. Others volunteer to escape abuse or exploitation at home. Some girls simply embrace it to be fed and clothed. In Sierra Leone, one young female member of the rebel army explained: "They offered me a choice of shoes and dresses. I never had decent shoes before."[5]

- *Inadequate verification procedures to determine the age of new recruits* in some countries also means that under-age soldiers are likely to be serving in security forces.

The Consequences

- Child soldiers are deprived of their childhood, normal social interaction and educational opportunities; sometimes, even, their lives. The traumas they experience often leave them with long-term guilt, shame, low self-esteem, nightmares and depression. Trained to forget home and family, some never find their way back to their villages. Girls who do they are likely to be rejected as "spoiled," whether or not they were forcibly conscripted.

- Children wounded in combat may be abandoned, or unable to get adequate medical treatment. Loss of limbs or deafness and blindness are most common. A high number of girls who have suffered sexual violence are left with AIDS or other diseases. Some have the additional care of children to whom they have given birth, and who are also stigmatized. Few countries have an adequate reintegration program for ex-child soldiers and they are not equipped to deal with such massive problems.

▶**Sudan** is recognized as having one of the worst records of child soldiers, forcibly recruiting many thousands as young as 12. A 2011 report by the National Council for Child Welfare said the Sudan Peoples' Liberation Army (SPLA) had recently snatched 900 children from their families and sent them to military training camps. In the years following the signing of a peace agreement in 2005 three thousand children were released; the army pledged to release the remaining thousands by 2014.[6]

▶90% of **Northern Uganda's** ill-named "Lord's Resistance Army (LRA)" led by Joseph Kony is composed of minors, over a third of them girls. More than 30,000 children have been systematically abducted during the last 25 years. In 2003, 45 children were drowned when they were forced into a river to test its depth. At least 591 more children were abducted between 2009 and 2012 and recruitment continues unabated.[7]

▶Islamists in the West African nation of **Mali** are buying children to serve as child soldiers, paying families $600 per child, according to an official from the United Nations.[8] Massive numbers were also recruited in 2012 by the national army of **Chad.**

▶UNICEF expressed concern over the increasing numbers of children being recruited by rebels and pro-government militias in the **Central African Republic** in 2013. Even before the most recent violence began in the country, some 2,500 children were part of armed groups.

▶In Latin America, **Colombia** has up to 14,000 children involved in militant groups, a quarter of them girls. In **Sri Lanka**, young Tamil girls, often orphans, were systematically conscripted by Tamil Tiger opposition fighters from the mid-1980's. And in **Nepal** both armed Maoist and government forces recruited, abducted, and tortured children.

▶In February 2013, **United States** President Barack Obama effectively nullified the Child Soldiers Protection Act (CSPA) of 2008. This law was passed unanimously by Congress as a deterrent to U.S. arms sales in countries determined by the State Department to be the worst abusers of child soldiers in their military. The CSPA made it a federal crime to recruit or to use soldiers under the age of 15. It gave the U.S. the authority to prosecute, deport, and deny entry to anybody who recruited child soldiers, and it also forbade the export arms and military items to countries that allowed use of child soldiers.

In spite of this, the Obama administration waved sanctions against certain countries in 2010 and again in 2011. His latest memo stated that he has determined that it's not in the national interest of the U.S. to proceed with this [CSPA], and therefore he has waived the application of this law with respect to certain nations like Libya, South Sudan, Yemen, and partially, in the case of Congo.[9]

ACTION STEPS

Zero under 18 Campaign:[10] In 2010, the Office of the Special Representative of the Secretary-General for Children and Armed Conflict along with United Nations partners launched a campaign to achieve universal ratification of the Optional Protocol to the Convention on the Rights of the Child on the Involvement of Children in Armed Conflict (OPAC). One of the objectives is to encourage all States to raise the age of voluntary recruitment to a minimum of 18 years. Find out more, including which countries have not signed or not ratified this protocol, at the campaign website www.zerounder18.org. If your government hasn't signed, write to your representatives.

Take a look at the fundraising ideas to help take girls out of uniform and into schools, at www.warchild.org.uk.

"O Lord, how long will you look on? Rescue my life from their ravages, my precious life from these lions." Psalm 35:17

(Endnotes)

1   Girls With Guns: An agenda on child soldiers for "Beijing Plus Five" COALITION TO STOP THE USE OF CHILD SOLDIERS, UK. *http://www.essex.ac.uk/armedcon/themes/child_soldiers/index.html*
2   Ibid.
3   http://www.child-soldiers.org/global_report_reader.php?id=97
4   http://www.amnesty.org.nz/files/Child-soldiers-factsheet.pdf
5   http://www.lalkar.org/issues/contents/jul2000/Sierraleone.htm
6   http://learningenglish.voanews.com/content/south-sudans-army-promises-to-release-child-soldiers-142998905/608797.html
7   http://smallwarsjournal.com/jrnl/art/youth-lost-ugandan-child-soldiers-in-the-lord%E2%80%99s-resistance-army
8   http://www.havocscope.com/price-to-buy-child-soldier-in-mali/
9   http://www.mnnonline.org/article/18196
10 http://www.zerounder18.org/

SOS: Girls on the Streets

At least *150 million children* now live and/or work on the streets of our world. They can be found in both developed and developing countries. They shelter under bridges, in landfills, train stations, ruined buildings and parks of our major cities. They may have family connections or they may be abandoned, evicted because there are too many mouths to feed, orphaned by war or by natural disasters. Often they have run away from bad situations only to confront worse: police violence, trafficking, forced labor or sex, exposure to HIV and other infections, drugs and gangs. Uneducated, unprotected and exploited, the average life expectancy of a child on the streets is four years.

Sex Tourism

Whether you're a businessman attending a conference in Vienna or taking a holiday in Thailand, Mexico or most other parts of the world, sexual services can be included in the hotel package. Engaging in child sex tourism (CST) in another country offers anonymity and access to underage partners. In fact, the average age of victims keeps decreasing; even involving very small children and babies. Girls on the streets are prime targets. In coastal resort areas of the Dominican Republic, child sex tourists arrive year-round from the United States and Europe. Costa Rica has an estimated 10,000 to 20,000 women and young girls servicing 25,000 to 50,000 sex tourists each year from North America. Rather than suppressing this highly profitable industry, the government has legalized prostitution. South Asia has long been a favored destination for CST, and Africa is also seeing an influx of European tourists seeking sex with children. Minors can be trafficked across country borders for use in sex tourism. In some cases, customers film episodes of exploitation to sell as child pornography. Some governments are making an effort to address the issue. Brazil, for instance, has implemented a national awareness campaign and Italy requires tour operators to inform travelers regarding its law on child sex offenses. But the growing popularity of sex tourism continues to snare hundreds of thousands of underage girls on the streets, every year.

AIDS Orphans

UNAIDS estimates that there are 16.6 million children who have been orphaned by AIDS, 90 percent of whom live in sub-Saharan Africa. Many of these children become homeless, forced to drop out of school. Teenage girls who take responsibility for younger siblings sometimes turn to "survival sex" to support them. Orphaned girls are three times more likely to be infected with HIV than girls who have parents. They are also far more likely to be abused.

> **Worldwide, nearly 50 percent of all sexual assaults are against girls aged 15 or younger. [WHO]**

Children's "Shelters"

Girls who are not actually on the streets but in care homes established to protect them are also at risk. A recent Asian Center for Human Rights report on "India's Hell Holes"[1] states that during the decade of 2001 to 2011, well over 48,000 children were raped in juvenile justice homes, shelters and orphanages. The actual number is unknown since many cases weren't reported to the police. Some of the attacks took place in private or NGO-run homes, others in government facilities. In the latter, perpetrators were members of staff including security guards, cooks and drivers, plus senior inmates and outsiders. India has hundreds of unregistered child care homes in spite of a requirement to register. Inspections are seldom carried out, allowing abuse and neglect to flourish. For the victims there is no escape.

Such exploitation isn't confined to India. In 2013 in Oxfordshire, England, a sex ring was exposed that had been preying on girls as young as 11 and 12 from children's homes. After picking the girls up they were raped or gang raped and sent to work in prostitution.[2]

GLOBAL SNAPSHOTS

THE AMERICAS

- **USA:** Each year 2.8 million teenagers run away from home. Within 24 hours of hitting the street, one-third are lured into prostitution or pornography. The National Center for Missing and Exploited Children estimates that one in five girls are sexually assaulted before they reach adulthood. Less than 35% of cases are reported to authorities.

- **Canada:** Runaways account for only a portion of the homeless youth population, which also includes young people living in shelters with their mother or both parents. A growing number of homeless minors are falling prey to pimps. In certain areas of British Colombia, aboriginal youth account for the majority of children working in the sex trade.

An estimated *50 million street children* live in Latin America. Many are victims of abuse, sometimes murder, by police and other authorities and individuals who are supposed to protect them.

- **Brazil** alone has approximately seven million street kids. Hundreds have been deliberately killed by "death squads" composed of active or former police, as a method of social cleansing.[3]

- **Bolivia:** 60% of street children here have left home because of violence. (UNICEF)

- UNICEF and other groups have jointly estimated that there are between 20,000 and 35,000 victims of child sexual exploitation in **Colombia**, with foreigners visibly seeking minors on the streets.

- 90% of boys and girls on **Guatemala's** streets have had contact with drugs, and been victims of some form of sexual abuse. (Conociendo)

- 16,000 children in **Mexico** are believed to be sexually exploited. (ECPAT)

- **Peru:** An estimated 250,000 children work on the city streets, six percent of them under six years old. 97% of kids use drugs. (Consortium for Street Children) Up to 10,000 street and underprivileged children die in the city of Lima every year.

- Of 143 homeless girls and boys interviewed in **Honduras**, 100% had at least one sexually transmitted disease, and 48.1% had been sexually abused by a member of their family. (Consortium for Street Children)

- About 44% of the estimated 2,300 prostitutes in three major red light districts of **San Salvador** are between the ages of 13 and 18. (Children of the Streets)

EUROPE

A half million girls and women from Central and Eastern Europe now serve as prostitutes in European Union nations.

- Traffickers find a ready source of young girls among orphanage "graduates" of **Eastern Europe**. Turned out to fend for themselves when they reach 16 or 17, these girls often don't have the skills to cope or find work. Within 48 hours of winding up on the streets most are picked up by Russian or Turkish mafia. Statistically, 90% of the girls will be prostituted, most against their will.

- Thousands of poor **Roma** boys and girls have been forced into streets across Europe by criminal gangs, to beg and steal. Madrid police say that 95% of children under 14 that they pick up stealing on the streets are Roma from Romania.[4]

- **Russia:** This country has about 1.2 million street kids. A large number take hazardous jobs to stay alive. Living in attics and basements, they go underground into giant pipes under the sity during the harsh winters, sniffing glue to help stay warm and distract from hunger. By age 11 most of these boys and girls are drug addicts. Eight percent have diseases or mental disorders. Russia has a seriously expanding HIV infection rate, mainly due to drug injection, which means that thousands of street children are also infected and untreated.

- **Ukraine:** Poverty, alcoholism and domestic violence have put at least 160,000 children onto the streets. Most homeless kids have one or more parents but they are unable or unwilling to take responsibility for them.

- **Romania:** UNICEF estimates that 350,000 children have been left behind by at least one parent who has gone to find a better job in the West. Thousands of such "migration orphans" also live in **Moldova**. Sometimes parents choose to remain away and even marry again. Children abandoned to very poor, overcrowded conditions without much adult supervision end up spending most of their time on the streets. They are extremely vulnerable to exploitation that includes sex tourism and trafficking.

- **France:** The charity France Terre d'Asile estimates that some 6,000 foreign children, many from Afghanistan and Bangladesh, risk their lives to travel illegally to France each year. Most turn up in Paris expecting to be able to work to send money home to their families. Since that is illegal they are faced with entering the black market or surviving on handouts.[5]

- **Germany:** Up to 20,000 children and youth live on the streets, at least short-term. In one of Europe's wealthiest countries poverty afflicts one in six children, according to statistics released by the German Society for the Protection of Children, and that is a factor. But some children run away from domestic violence or neglect in wealthy homes.[6]

- **Greece:** The economic meltdown has led to a growing number of Greek children being dumped on the streets by parents who cannot afford to care for them. Added to these are hundreds of homeless immigrant children. Other kids are trafficked to Greece, primarily from Albania and Romania, to work for bosses. Involvement of minors in the sex trade has tripled during the last decade. Prostitution is legal.

- **Great Britain:** Every five minutes a child runs away from home. Most of the 100,000 under-16's who leave home each year are fleeing neglect or abuse. Nobody knows the exact numbers living rough since they try to stay invisible. The UK has only a few shelters where kids under 16 can walk in off the street without an authority referral. Girls as young as 11 and 12 have been picked up and enslaved for the purpose of prostitution.

ASIA

Asia has always been a major hub of sex tourism and exploitation of children.

Philippines: One of the favored destinations of sex tourists from Europe and the United States. An estimated 1.5 million street children work as pickpockets, beggars, drug traffickers and prostitutes. Some 20,000 girls are victims of the latter in Metro Manila alone. (ECPAT)

Australia: 3,000 children work in the sex industry, some younger than 10. Girls work in brothels, escort work, street prostitution, pornography, sex for favors and stripping. Sex tourism and pedophilia is a serious problem.

It is estimated that between 15 to 20% of street children in **Vietnam** are HIV positive. (Consortium for Street Children)

One study estimated that there were 1000 children living on the street in Phnom Penh, **Cambodia**; another 15,000 live at home but spend six or more hours each day scavenging on the streets to earn money for their families. About 88% of vulnerable children had had sexual relations with tourists, finding that prostitution made a lot more money in much less time. Girls in Cambodia who live on the streets don't last long: they are soon sold to brothels. (Consortium for Street Children) Only about five percent of **Nepal's** 5,000 street kids are girls and their job is usually to look after younger ones. In Pokara, 90% of such girls were found to be sexually abused by hotel and restaurant owners, people in places of work, older boys in their group, friends and other locals. (Plan International)

India: Of *ten million* street children, one out of every ten are girls. Many of them will die of AIDS or simply "disappear."

AFRICA

- The majority of street kids in **South Africa** are between the ages of 13 and 16. Police in Durban have found girls as young as 12 years old selling their bodies on the streets.

- Around one million children are believed to be on the streets of **Egypt**, mostly in Cairo and Alexandria and mainly because of abuse at home. (Consortium for Street Children)

- **Senegal:** An estimated 20,000 children are sent out as beggars by their Muslim Qur'anic master in the Dakar region.[7]

- The **Democratic Republic of the Congo**, in spite of its huge natural resources and potential for riches, is one of Africa's poorest countries. Of almost 250,000 street boys and girls, 70,000 live in Kinshasa, the capital city. Some leave home to escape abusive treatment, others are conscripted to fight in rebel groups and then left stranded.[8]

- **Kenya:** An estimated 250,000 to 300,000 children live on the streets, and a UNICEF report says that a staggering 30% or more of children between 12 and 18 are involved in the sex tourism business. Some 30,000 girls aged from 12 to 14 are sexually exploited in hotels and private villas. (ECPAT)

- Many children in the Niger Delta of **Nigeria** have been accused of witchcraft in recent years. Over 95% of the children on the streets of Akwa Ibom State have been stigmatized as "witches" by pastors and abandoned to live on the streets by their parents. These boys and girls are often beaten, tortured and sexually abused by the public and police.[9]

Action Steps:

The **International Day for Street Children** is observed every year on April 12th. Why not use this day to draw attention to the lack of rights of children on the street? Viva Network's **World Weekend of Prayer** for children at risk is another opportunity, held every year over the first weekend of June. Viva is helping organizations to network more effectively. See Appendix 2 for websites and ways you can get involved.

"Whoever shuts their ears to the cry of the poor will also cry out and not be answered." Proverbs 21:13

(Endnotes)

1 http://www.achrweb.org/reports/india/IndiasHellHoles2013.pdf

2 http://www.independent.co.uk/voices/comment/how-could-so-many-years-of-horrendous-abuse-go-unnoticed-in-this-case-the-guilt-extends-way-beyond-oxford-sex-traffickers-8617339.html

3 http://www.independent.co.uk/news/world/americas/death-to-undesirables-brazils-murder-capital-1685214.html

4 http://news.bbc.co.uk/1/hi/8226580.stm

5 http://www.cnn.com/2012/05/17/world/europe/afghan-street-kids-in-paris

6 http://www.expatica.com/de/news/local_news/Growing-number-of-street-children-in-Germany_-report-says—_3618.html

7 http://www.globalgiving.org/projects/unite-and-educate-10-street-kids-in-dakar-senegal/

8 http://www.asafeworldforwomen.org/partners-in-africa/partners-in-drc/cofapri/cofapri-blogs/1749-drc-street-children.html

9 http://www.steppingstonesnigeria.org/street-children.html

SOS: Health and Life Expectancy

In poor areas, the health of women and girls is often at the bottom of the priority list for government attention. Life spans are dramatically shortened for the millions born in developing nations, largely due to the following preventable problems.

Lack of access to safe water

783 million people worldwide live without the privilege of safe drinking water, according to the UN. Water-related diseases are the second biggest killer of children, taking a life every eight seconds. About five million men, women and children die each year after drinking unsafe water. The following are just some of the possible consequences:

- *Schistosomiasis* [also called *bilharzia*] is a parasitic disease largely caused by infested surface water, endemic in 74 countries. The World Health Organization (WHO)* reported that **243 million people** required treatment for this in 2011. Some 20 million suffered severe consequences such as renal failure or bladder cancer.

- *Trachoma* has blinded six million people. Studies show that an adequate water supply could reduce trachoma infections by **25 percent.**

- *Typhoid fever*, annually affecting about 12 million people, is a bacterial infection caused by ingesting contaminated food or water.

- *Fluorosis* is a serious bone disease caused by high concentrations of fluoride occurring naturally in groundwater. It is endemic in at least 25 countries across the globe, affecting tens of millions.

Tuberculosis. *Second only to HIV/AIDS as the greatest killer worldwide due to a single infectious agent.* This illness is among the top three causes of death for women aged 15 to 44, and a leading killer among those living with HIV. An estimated 8.7 million fell ill with tuberculosis in 2011. In some parts of the world, the stigma attached to TB also leads to isolation, abandonment and divorce.

Malaria takes the life of a child every minute in Africa, although it is preventable and curable. It also causes high rates of miscarriage in pregnant women, and maternal death rates of 10 to 50%. Malarial anemia is estimated to cause as many as 10,000 maternal deaths each year.

Action Steps

Mark World Malaria Day [www.worldmalariaday.org] on 25 April and help defeat this global killer. Share reports, images, video and other media with your friends, available for download from the Malaria Consortium [www.malariaconsortium.org]. Support the "Nothing But Nets" campaign [http://nothingbutnets.net], a grassroots effort raising funds to "send a net and save a life."

Measles is the most contagious disease known to man and leading childhood killer in developing countries, accounting for about 900,000 deaths per year. Yet one in every four children in these countries is not immunized against measles.

NUTRITION

Undernourishment kills more people every year than malaria, tuberculosis and AIDS combined. [USAID] An inadequate diet stunts the growth of one in four children in developing countries.

Vitamin Deficiencies

- *Vitamin D deficiency retards the growth* of 30% of children in China, South Asia and Africa, according to WHO; it also reduces their resistance to disease and makes them vulnerable to mental health disorders. A large percentage of Chinese and Mongolian children have developed **rickets**, a disease that softens the bones, because of a deficiency of vitamin D.

- *Vitamin A: Every year an estimated 670,000 children will die and 350,000 will go blind* because of the lack of a small amount of vitamin A in their diet. Helen Keller International has estimated that 4.4 million preschool children are already blind from this deficiency, 40% of them in India. Vitamin A deficiency also increases the risk of maternal mortality.

- *Iron:* Over 30% of the world's population—a staggering two billion people—are **anemic**, mainly due to iron deficiency. Severe iron deficiency anemia is the cause of 20% of **maternal deaths.**

- *Iodine deficiency* is a leading global cause of preventable **mental retardation and brain damage.**

CHILD & INFANT MORTALITY

Each day **10,000** babies are born dead, and 10,000 newborns die within a month of birth. More than nine million die each year before their fifth birthday, over one-third because of *malnutrition.* Six million of these child deaths are preventable. In Sub-Saharan Africa, one in eight children die before their fifth birthday—nearly 20 times the average for developed regions. [UNICEF]

Diarrhea has killed more children in the past 10 years than all the people killed by armed conflicts since World War II. It remains the second leading cause of death for children under five, killing 1.8 million children each year. [UNICEF]

Countries with the highest infant mortality are **Afghanistan** with 119 deaths for every 1000 live births, then **Niger** (108 deaths) **Mali** (107 deaths), **Somalia** (102) and **Central African Republic** (95). Compare these high death rates with Monaco—only 1.8 deaths per 1000 births and Japan with only 2.2, closely followed by Bermuda, Singapore and Sweden. [Geoba.se, 2013 estimates]

LIFE EXPECTANCY for WOMEN*
"2013 Estimates"

10 Lowest Countries		10 Highest Countries	
South Africa	48.5	Monaco	93.8
Swaziland	49	Macau	87.5
Chad	49.8	Japan	87.4
Afghanistan	51	Singapore	86.2
Guinea Bissau	51.1	San Marino	85.8
Zimbabwe	51.7	Hong Kong	85.1
Central African Republic	51.8	Guernsey	85.
Namibia	51.9	Andorra	84.7
Lesotho	52	France	84.7
Mozambique	52.8	Italy	84.6

*Source: *CIA World Factbook, 2012*

COUNTRY CLOSE-UPS

Afghanistan: One of the most dangerous places in the world to be a pregnant woman or a young child. Every 30 minutes, an Afghan woman dies during childbirth. Afghan women also suffer one of the world's highest rates of tuberculosis. One in every three women experience physical, psychological or sexual violence. 70% to 80% face forced marriages. [WHO & Integrated Regional Information Networks]

Cameroon: One in four females is subjected to "breast ironing" or "breast flattening," the pounding and massaging of a pubescent girl's breasts, using hard or heated objects, to try to make them stop developing or disappear. Since girls whose breasts have started to grow are considered ready for sex in some areas, mothers who carry out the practice say it is a way to prevent their daughters from harassment or early pregnancy; they are simply protecting the family's honor. The most widely used implement for breast ironing is a wooden pestle normally used for pounding food. Other tools used include leaves, bananas, coconut shells, grinding stones, ladles, spatulas, and hammers heated over coals.[1]

China: Due to the ongoing "one child" policy, neglect of female offspring is dramatically apparent. According to WHO: "In many cases, mothers are more likely to bring their male children to health centers—particularly to private physicians —and they may be treated at an earlier stage of disease than girls." Pregnant women in China have been forced to undergo abortions in even their eighth and ninth months. *[See also "Vital Statistics — Female Infanticide and Feticide"]*

India: UN data in 2012 shows India to be the most dangerous place in the world to be a baby girl. An Indian female aged one to five years is 75% more likely to die than an Indian boy. UNICEF says that almost 55 million children under the age of five in India are underweight. In a great many Indian homes, females are the last members of the family to eat. Often they survive on leftovers. Almost half of Indian women aged 15 to 49 are anemic because of poor nutrition, which leads to extremely high maternal death rates.[2] *[See also "Vital Statistics - Childbirth"]*

Uzbekistan: According to reports by a number of sources in 2011 and 2012, including the BBC and Moscow Times, forced abortion and coerced sterilization are current government policy in Uzbekistan for women with two or three children, as a means of forcing population control and improving maternal mortality rates.[3]

*Note: Much of the information in this section comes from the World Health Organization

(Endnotes)
1 http://lindaraftree.com/2012/06/14/new-research-on-the-practice-of-breast-flattening-in-cameroon/
2 http://health.india.com/diseases-conditions/international-womens-day-2013-arent-you-ashamed-to-be-indian/
3 http://www.bbc.co.uk/programmes/b01fjx63;http://www.themoscowtimes.com/news/article/uzbeks-face-forced-sterilization/401279.html

SOS: "Honor" Killings — Getting Away with Murder

Between 5,000 and 20,000 women each year die at the hands of relatives who find their behavior inappropriate or unacceptable. The true number of "honor" killings worldwide is hard to determine since most deaths are made to look like accidents. Victims have been stoned, stabbed, suffocated, burned, beheaded, electrocuted and even buried alive. Their so-called crimes may be as petty as dating without permission or simply talking to a man or even cooking badly. In cultures where men go unpunished for overtly illicit relationships, women die for the faintest rumor of impropriety. Even victims of rape may be eliminated by families who feel they've been shamed. Killings have been reported in 26 countries, most often in Muslim-majority cultures but also in Hindu, Sikh and Christian communities.

The following are representative incidents of "honor" killings:

▶An **Egyptian** bride on her honeymoon was attacked by her father for marrying a man he didn't approve. After cutting off her head, he proudly paraded it down the street.

▶A mother in **Pakistan** was sleeping next to her three-month-old baby when her husband shot and killed her. A neighbor had informed him he'd seen a man near the field where she was working.

▶ In March 2012, Reuters reported that near the northern **Iraqi** city of Kirkuk, a father doused his three teenage daughters with boiling water and shot them. Two of the three died. In his defense, the man told a court he suspected the girls were having sex. Medical examinations showed that they were virgins.[1] He received a two year sentence. An Iraqi Human Rights ministry report said 249 women were murdered in 2010, many for "honor crimes."

▶A young woman in **Jordan** ran away to marry the man she loved, without the family's permission. A few years later her sister also ran away to join her. Their brothers found out where the girls were living, went into their home with axes and hacked both sisters to death. The incident came only a day after Jordan's parliament rejected a bill that would impose tougher sentences for such crimes.

Some Jordanian women have chosen to remain in prison after serving a criminal sentence, rather than return home and face violence or death at the hands of their families.

▶In the **UK**, police recorded over 2,800 "honor" attacks in 2011, up 47 percent from previous years.[2] On the average, at least one woman dies every month. These crimes occur almost exclusively within Asian or Middle Eastern families, often when their women seek greater independence or seemingly embrace Western values. They may, for instance, refuse an arranged marriage or wear Western clothing. In Great Britain the perpetrators are prosecuted but in some countries such killings are culturally acceptable and killers may receive only a light sentence or none at all (see section below on laws in various countries).

▶Ignoring the pleas of his 14-year old daughter to spare her life, Mehmet Halitogullari in **Turkey** wrapped a wire around her neck and strangled her—supposedly to restore the family's honor after she was kidnapped and raped. "I decided to kill her because our honor was dirtied," the newspaper *Sabah* quoted the father as saying. One thousand women were murdered in 2009, most stabbed or shot by family members. Women's rights groups believe a large proportion were "honor" killings.

▶"Every year about 40 **Palestinian** women die at the hands of their fathers or brothers," writes Geraldine Brooks in her book, *Nine Parts of Desire;* "they are accused of pre-marital or extra-marital sex. Often the women are then burned so the killing is passed off as an accident. The killer becomes a local hero."[3]

▶So-called honor crimes are probably most common in **Pakistan.** At least 943 women were murdered in 2011 for allegedly defaming their family's honor, according to the Human Rights Commission of Pakistan. The death rate is growing each year as more women seek divorce from abusive husbands. Incidents of women being permanently disfigured from acid attacks became so common that in 2010, Pakistan's parliament was at last driven to address the problem by passing an "Acid Control and Acid Crime Prevention Bill." However, only about ten percent of cases make it to court and most attackers escape punishment by paying off authorities.[4]

Virginity Restoration

So harsh is the punishment of Muslim girls who lose their virginity before their wedding night that many now seek surgery to repair the telltale signs. In fact, Britain's National Health Service includes this procedure in its range of free care services, funded by taxpayers. Other girls undergo the operation at private health clinics at a cost of up to $6000.[5] One Harley Street doctor says they get two or three of such patients a day. The phenomenon is not limited to the UK, however. A check online reveals that the procedure is openly offered in other places like India and Iran, and it is very likely carried out secretly in a majority of countries.

LAWS REGARDING
"CRIMES OF HONOR" IN ARAB STATES

Arab penal codes in a number of countries continue to directly violate women's rights in two major areas: leniency for those accused of "honor crimes" and waivers of charges against rapists who marry their victims.

Most of the laws below concern the treatment of those who murder or wound others after finding them in the act of adultery with their partner or spouse. In many cases the murderer is either exempt from punishment or given very short sentences. Killings committed over other situations perceived as immoral are not discussed. [See also VITAL STATISTICS - Gender Inequalities]

▶**ALGERIA**

"Murder, wounding and beating shall be subject to excuse if committed by one spouse against the other spouse or against his/her partner at the moment of surprising them in the act of adultery." [Penal Code Article 279]

▶**IRAQ**

Article 409 of this government's constitution reduces a murder sentence to a maximum of three years if a man "surprises his wife or one of his female dependents (who is) in a state of adultery or finds her in bed with a partner and kills her immediately, or kills one of them." However, families often cover up such crimes, presenting deaths as suicides or accidents, and courts are lenient.

The law absolutely absolves from liability a man who kills or attempts to kill another person who has raped or forced a blood relative of the killer to have sexual intercourse with him. Further and by way of protection to the killer, should he become the victim of revenge, such revenge will be deemed an aggravating circumstance.

The article also provides that when a man kills his wife or a blood relative by reason of a crime of honor, and then kills another person who taunts the killer and imputes dishonor, then the second crime will be deemed to be subject to an extenuating circumstance. Anyone who kills the said avenger will be subject to a death sentence.

▶**JORDAN**

This country gives reduced sentences to men who kill their wives or female family members if they have brought dishonor to their family. Sometimes families use their under 18-year-old sons to commit the crimes, since convicted minors only serve time in a juvenile detention center and are released with a clean criminal record at the age of 18.

"He who discovers his wife or one of his female unlawfuls committing adultery with another, and he kills, wounds, or injures one or both of them, is exempt from any penalty. He who catches his wife, or one of his female ascendants or descendants or sisters with another in an unlawful bed and he kills or wounds or injures one or both of them, benefits from a reduction in penalty." [Penal Code Article 340]

Article 98 of the code has also been invoked for "honor" killings. This mandates reduction of penalty for a perpetrator who commits a crime in a "state of great fury" resulting from an unlawful and dangerous act on the part of the victim. *It is not necessary that the murder be provoked by any actual proof* of sexual indiscretion; in practice, mere suspicion or rumor of a woman's "unlawful and dangerous" act may be sufficient proof for the courts. Punishment may therefore be waived or reduced to a nominal three to six months in jail.

▶**KUWAIT**

"He who surprises his wife in the act of adultery or surprises his daughter, mother or sister in the act of sexual intercourse with a man, and immediately kills her or the man who is committing adultery or having sex with her or kills both of them, shall be punished by prison for a period *not more than three years* and a fine of not more than 3000 dinars or by one of these two penalties. [Penal Code Article 153]

▶**LIBYA**

"Whosoever surprises his wife, daughter, sister or mother in the act of adultery or in illegitimate sexual intercourse and immediately kills her or her partner or both in response to the assault that has affected his honor or the honor of his family, shall be punished by a prison sentence. If the act leads to grave or serious injury of the said persons in these circumstances, the penalty shall be prison for *not more than two years*. Mere beating or light injury in such circumstances shall not be penalized." [Penal Code Article 375]

▶**MOROCCO**

"Murder, injury and beating are excusable if they are committed by a

husband on his wife as well as the accomplice at the moment in which he surprises them in the act of adultery. [Penal Code Article 418]

▶**OMAN**

"He who surprises his wife committing adultery or surprises his mother or his sister or his daughter in an unlawful bed, and immediately kills or injures her or kills or injures the person committing adultery with her or in the bed with her, or kills or injures both of them, *may be exempted from liability or be liable to a reduced penalty* according to the provisions of article 109 of this law." [Penal Code Article 252]

▶**PALESTINIAN AUTHORITY**

In the Gaza Strip and West Bank, it is believed that three to four women are killed every month in the name of saving honor. The Palestinian Authority follows the Jordanian law, which gives men reduced punishment for killing wives or female relatives if they have brought dishonor to the family.[6]

▶**SYRIA**

Under Syrian law, an "honor" killing has long been considered to offer "mitigating circumstances" for murder. A new law in 2009, however, eliminated Article 548 of the Penal Code, which withheld punishment for men who were found guilty of "honor" killing, and called for a minimum jail term of two years.

However, Article 192 of the Syrian penal code facilitates the acquittal of honor crime committers, providing judges with a number of options for reduced sentences, like short-term detention or imprisonment, in cases of killings which are based on an honorable intent. Finally, Article 242 of the code allows judges to reduce the punishment of both women and men if a murder was committed in rage and motivated by any illegal act on the part of the victim.

Activists say some 200 women are killed each year in honor cases by men who expect lenient treatment under the law.

▶**YEMEN**

"If a husband kills his wife and whoever is fornicating with her at the moment of their adultery, or if he attacks them in a manner that leads to death or disability, no option of *qisas*[7] arises; the husband shall be penalised by imprisonment for a period of not more than one year *or by a fine.* This ruling applies also to a person who surprises one of

his ascendants, descendants or sisters in the act of illicit fornication."
[Article 232 of law no.12/1994]

Action Steps

Check out the "Gendercide" website and "Stop Honour Killings" campaigns; websites are listed in Appendix 2 under "Honor" Killings. You can also refer friends to the Facebook page: International Campaign Against Honour Killings.

"But the Lord is still in his holy temple; he still rules from heaven. He closely watches everything that happens here on earth. He puts the righteous and the wicked to the test; he hates those loving violence."
Psalm 11:4,5; The Living Bible

(Endnotes)
1   http://www.womenagainstshariah.com/2012/03/honor-killings-require-tougher-laws-say.html
2   http://www.bbc.co.uk/news/uk-16014368
3   Geraldine Brooks, Nine Parts of Desire (New York, Doubleday, 1995), p.49.
4   http://www.bbc.co.uk/news/world-asia-17676542
5   http://www.dailymail.co.uk/news/article-1298684/Surge-virginity-repair-operations-NHS.html
6   http://articles.timesofindia.indiatimes.com/2010-07-11/india/28318807_1_honour-killings-family-honour-reports-by-human-rights
7   *Qisas* refer to physical retaliation for wounds inflicted or in the case of an intentional murder, the putting to death of the murderer.

SOS: Poverty

Women represent a disproportionate percentage of the world's poor, and they are also the fastest growing group of impoverished. Almost half the global population lives on less than $2 a day and 1.2 billion people live in absolute poverty, having extreme difficulty just to survive on less than $1.25 a day. Seventy percent are women.

One person in eight battles hunger. 24,000 die daily from hunger and three-fourths are children under five. Another 925 million people are chronically undernourished; over 25 percent of all children in developing countries are underweight.

- Approximately 1.3 billion have no reliable access to electricity and an estimated 2.7 billion people will not have access to adequate sanitation by 2015.

- Seventy percent of the poorest people in developing countries live in rural areas, and women are particularly disadvantaged. If they had the same access to land, technology, financial services, education and markets as men, the number of hungry people could be reduced by 100-150 million.

- The economic situation for women in many developing societies often sharply deteriorates when they are elderly, widowed or disabled, because they lack support systems. Destitute women become most vulnerable to all types of abuse and exploitation.

[Sources: World Food Programme, FAO, IFAD, UNICEF, WHO, UN]

Homelessness

Nobody knows how many people worldwide have no place to call home, but estimates place numbers at 100 to 200 million. 33 percent of women across the globe are either homeless or living in inadequate dwellings, such as slums. There has also been a sharp rise in female-headed households—about 33 percent globally, and up to 45 and 50 percent in some parts of Africa and Latin America. Yet women are less likely to have steady employment, and most likely to be paid less than male counterparts. Because they lack permanent employment and title deeds to land or housing to offer as security, some 75 percent of the world's women cannot get formal bank loans. [Shelter 2.0]

Poverty, unemployment and lack of affordable housing are three major reasons for the growing numbers sleeping rough in cities. Europe is no exception. London alone has some 6,400 living on the streets—double the number of six years ago. Women in this situation include immigrants, sex workers and women in unstable jobs—even professionals. Few if any countries have enough crisis shelters or centers.

Spreading Slums

One billion people—one in every seven of us—live in a slum. The trend for moving from rural to urban areas has meant that cities are growing by 200,000 new residents every day. The UN estimates that by 2030 two billion will live in slums. Those who fail to find jobs usually end up as squatters in settlements crowded with poor quality hovels with inadequate sanitation, unsafe water and no security for the future. Women often bear the brunt of the suffering in order to provide for their families.

Descent-based Slavery

Thousands of people in **West Africa** today are born into a slave class or caste of a society, considered by others to be on the bottom of the social ladder. Usually this kind of slavery has existed for generations and is deeply imbedded. The members of such groups are discriminated against, not allowed to inherit or own property or marry outside the slave caste. Children of such unions belong to their masters, who can give them away as they choose. Although slavery was made a criminal offence in **Niger** in 2003, many young girls and women of slave descent are sold by their masters to become concubines and slaves to wealthy men, known as "*Wahaya*" or "fifth wives." In **Mauritania**, hundreds of thousands of poor Hratine people make up the main "slave caste," usually owned by the ethnic elite White Moors. Women face double discrimination both as members of the caste and as women, frequently beaten and raped by their masters. Descent-based slavery still exists in northern **Mali** as well, although the country formally abolished slavery in the 1960's. [Anti-Slavery Society]

India: 44 percent of people live below the $1 per day poverty line. India's Dalits, formerly called "untouchables," are the poorest of the poor and Dalit women are particularly oppressed. Many are forced into the most menial labor, like the manual cleaning of toilets. Over a million women have been employed in removing human excrement from dry toilets and sewers, for pennies a day. Only in August 2012 was the "Prohibition of Employment as Manual Scavengers and their Rehabilitation Bill passed by India's Parliament. Dalit women, however, continue to be denied their rights and are regularly and openly abused. Cases have even been found of removing the organs of Dalit women, like kidneys, without their knowledge or consent.

Migrant Workers

Female migrant workers have been increasing and now constitute 50 percent or more of the 214 million migrant workforce across the globe. According to UN Women, women usually leave home and become migrant workers to escape poverty but often find themselves deeply exploited. They routinely lack access to social services and legal protection and are subjected to abuses such as harsh working and living conditions, low wages, illegal withholding of wages and premature termination of employment, even though they may be sending money home to support families. [See also "Vital Statistics - Refugees"]

WORLD SNAPSHOTS

Women in *Africa* and *Asia* walk an average of six kilometers to obtain water. This necessity has resulted in many cases of permanent damage to their health, including spinal and pelvic deformities, and degenerative rheumatism. One flush of a toilet uses as much water as the average person in the developing world uses for a whole day's washing, cleaning, cooking and drinking.

Poverty can overtake no matter how hard one works. In *sub-Saharan Africa,* women are responsible for 70 to 80 percent of household food production. A huge proportion have manual jobs, and a very low percentage have skilled and high-paying work.

The bottom 12 countries in the latest UN Human Development Index, which measures overall health, education and income, are all in Africa. [UNDP]

Latin America and Caribbean countries have made strong economic gains that have reduced poverty rates, but needs are most problematic in rural areas, particularly among indigenous peoples. The gap between the very rich and very poor is noticeable.

Bolivia, Paraguay and Guyana are thought to be the three poorest countries in South America; **Haiti** remains the poorest in the Caribbean.

In *Europe* the economic recession has hit hard. The amount of food aid distributed to people in Europe by the Red Cross has reached levels not seen since World War II. **Bulgaria** and **Spain** have been particularly affected. Fuel poverty is also growing: In a **United Kingdom** survey of 1,000 families in 2013, one in four families had to choose between heating and eating. More people are dying as a result of living in a cold house in the winter than dying in road traffic accidents each year.

South Asia is home to the largest concentration of chronically poor people in the world. More than 500 million live on less than $1.25 a day, according to the World Bank. One third live in **India**, where 60 percent of women are chronically poor; most of the remainder are in **Nepal, Bangladesh** and **Pakistan**. Although a significant number work, these people are usually landless or near-landless and members of minorities—low status castes or tribes or religious minorities. Employment opportunities for women tend to be restricted.

At least 153 million dollars was spent today on weight loss products in the U.S. About 30 million dollars would have fed all of the earth's poorest citizens.

Action Steps

- Join WarOnWant.org campaigns that fight global poverty, like those calling for human rights for workers in factories and sweatshops.

- Many Christian missions would welcome your support for projects that empower impoverished women, such as microfinance schemes and job training.

- Check out www.WorldHunger.org and other websites for statistics, about world hunger—great for sharing with groups.

- Click thehungersite.org every day to give free food.

"Defend the cause of the weak and fatherless; maintain the rights of the poor and oppressed. Rescue the weak and needy...." Psalm 82:3,4

SOS: Rape as a Weapon of War and Religious Extremism

Over 70% of deaths in recent conflicts have been women and children, according to UN WOMEN: far outnumbering military casualties. Those who do manage to survive have often fallen prey to torture, rape, sexual slavery, enforced prostitution and mutilation.

Since the beginning of warfare, soldiers have considered themselves entitled to rape as part of the spoils of victory. But sexual assault has also evolved as an intentional, systematic tactic to terrorize the enemy during conflicts.

Either way, the consequences to victims continue long after peace accords are signed: displacement, unwanted pregnancies, sexually transmitted infections, psychological trauma and stigmatization. Girls who have been "shamed," even through no fault of their own, can expect rejection by their families, loss of further schooling and few employment options. They face a bleak future. Caring for children who are the result of rape presents additional difficulties.

Only in 2008 did the UN Security Council pass a resolution that declared rape and other forms of sexual violence a war crime, a crime against humanity, and a constitutive act with respect to genocide.

Appallingly, a UN task force found that some of the aid workers, peacekeepers and other local and foreign humanitarian staff of 23 organizations they studied *were themselves responsible for further exploitation.* Staff members committed "every kind of child sexual abuse and exploitation imaginable" with girls and women living in chronic emergency situations. Children as young as six were trading sex with aid workers and peacekeepers, for instance, in exchange for food, money, soap and other items.[1]

The examples below merely scratch the surface of the pervasive incidence of sexual violence during past and present warfare and unrest. Dozens more countries could be named, including Algeria, Bangladesh, Sri Lanka, Somalia and Uganda.

World War II

Japanese soldiers who invaded China raped local women on a massive scale in 1937 and 1938—some estimate up to 80,000. Hundreds of thousands more were kidnapped and used as "comfort women" by the

Japanese throughout the war years. Russian troops raped an estimated two million women in revenge for casualties inflicted by the Germans.

Rwanda

Between 250,000 to 500,000 women and girls were raped in the 1994 Rwandan genocide, many of them suffering multiple attacks after being forced to witness the murder of their loved ones. Mutilation and torture often followed. The approximately 20,000 children who were conceived from these brutal assaults—along with their mothers—were mostly shunned. Often both mothers and children were also infected with HIV.

Sudan: Darfur

The United Nations reports that Sudan's government forces and Janjaweed militias abducted thousands of civilians from Darfur refugee camps for sex slavery and forced labor. Kidnapped women and girls as young as four years old were repeatedly raped as well as forced to perform chores for the fighters. The violence reached a peak from 2003-2006. Scores of babies born as a result were abandoned by mothers trying to escape the stigma. Other females were sold into forced marriages with soldiers. Assaults continue as of this writing.

The Democratic Republic of the Congo (DRC)

This country vies with South Africa as the rape capital of the world. Approximately 1.7 to 1.8 million women reported having been raped in their lifetime. More than 1,100 women suffered sexual assault every day during a 12-month period in 2006 and 2007: more than 400,000 women and girls between the ages of 15 to 49. Six percent were younger than 16 years and 10% were older than 65 years. A 2011 report indicated that sexual violence against civilians is ongoing in the East of the country, with up to 25,000 rapes per year, perpetrated by both government security forces and militias.[2] Many victims are gang-raped. Since raped women are considered impure, this frequently means no one will marry them or they are abandoned by their husbands. The victim is sometimes even killed by her family or community if they believe that she has brought them dishonor.

Balkan Conflicts

According to a report by the Council of Europe, more than 20,000 women were molested during the Bosnia and Herzegovina and Kosovo wars in the 90's, most of them gang-raped. Some victims were forced into sexual slavery and forcibly impregnated, often by armies and paramilitary groups, as part of their system of ethnic cleansing.[3]

2012 and 2013

Amnesty International reported that rapes by soldiers and members of armed groups occurred and still occur in many conflict zones, including **Mali, Chad, Sudan** and the **DRC**. Rape survivors have been stigmatized by their communities and not given adequate support or assistance. UNICEF noted that systematic rape and sexual violence is being perpetrated against women and children in **Myanmar (Burma)** as a method of torture and control, often by military officers or with their complicity. A study in the minority Shan state found that 61% of the rape incidents documented involved gang rape. The attacks were witnessed but since they were committed collectively, soldiers had no fear of repercussions.[4]

Female Serving Soldiers in the U.S.

While statistics are not available about what happens in other countries, a recent documentary has exposed the fact that over 500,000 female soldiers have been sexually assaulted while serving in the American military. The number of assaults reported to the Public Defence in 2010 was over 19,000. According to this department, one in three women are sexually assaulted during their military service. Countless cases are hidden behind walls of secrecy.[5]

The Vulnerability of Refugee Women

Girls and women survivors of sexual violence find that legal remedies are all too often inaccessible to them, ineffective or untrustworthy. Knowing that justice systems do not protect women and children allows assailants to behave with impunity. Often unprotected females in refugee camps are attacked in their temporary shelters, many of which do not have doors or locks. "Survival sex" results when victims who are shamed by rape and forced out of their families and communities see no other option for obtaining food and clothing. Their bodies are the only possession they have to sell.

In addition, medical treatment for women and girls who have suffered rape is often inadequate or unavailable. The confidentiality of rape victims who seek medical treatment may also be in question.[6]

RAPE AND RELIGIOUS EXTREMISM

The last few decades have reflected a disturbing increase in rape as a strategy to humiliate women of minority faiths and forcibly make converts. In Muslim countries where the female sex does not traditionally enjoy the privileges accorded to male citizens, Christian women are even more at risk as members of an "infidel," outcast population.[7] This trend has been obvious in many countries but we will take a brief look at three of them.

- **Nigeria:** For years the extreme Islamist group Boko Haram has struck fear into Christian hearts by kidnapping women. Muslims say that a wife must follow the religion of her husband, so this is interpreted as a free license to kidnap Christian girls for rape and forced marriage. The girls' religious status is then changed from Christian to Muslim on their identity cards.

- **Egypt:** Over 500 Christian girls have been abducted since the 2011 revolution by Salafists (extreme Sunni Muslims) who forcibly convert the girls to Islam and then marry them to Muslim men against their will. These cases have been documented by the non-governmental Christian organization Association of Victims of Abduction and Enforced Disappearance (AVAED), which states that Egypt's interior ministry colluded with the kidnappings. AVAED lawyer Said Fayez observed that the age of the abducted girls is becoming younger, typically 13-14 years old. [Barnabas Fund]

- **Pakistan:** Along with low-caste females, Pakistan's Christian minority has long been targeted for brutal and degrading treatment. In the last several years a number of incidents have been reported (many more go unreported) of humiliating, torturing and parading Christian women through the streets. Young girls are also molested. Local police usually turn a blind eye to such incidents.

Western Nations

Religious bigotry and hatred has also been driving an alarming escalation of sexual attacks in the developed world. In Australia, for instance, a Pakistani-born rapist testified in a New South Wales Supreme Court that his victims had no right to say no [to forced sex], because they were not wearing a headscarf. A Muslim scholar in

Copenhagen, Shahid Mehdi, stated much the same thing, that women who did not wear a headscarf were asking to be raped.

Norway and Sweden have experienced a virtual rape epidemic in recent years. Two out of three perpetrators in Oslo, police report, are immigrants with a non-western background; 80 percent of their victims are Norwegian women. Gang rapes in Sweden are most usually committed by Muslim immigrant males with native Swedish girls. Assailants often give their motives as a desire for conquest or to humiliate and dishonor their victims or Christian communities. Sometimes they are incited to act by extremist sermons or Islamic leaders. It has been argued that rape could really be classified as a hate crime rather than sex crime, that the motive is often power, not passion.

Action Steps

Learn more about the work of the International Justice Mission (IJM) [www.ijm.org], which actively rescues victims of sexual violence, secures evidence and ensures aftercare services for women and their families. The IJM also works to transform justice systems in many countries. Speakers are available to UK and U.S. churches or communities. See their fundraising tool kit for ideas like sponsored runs, car washes or bake sales. Get behind their advocacy campaigns.

"For traumatic experiences, 'forgetting' is impossible, yet remembering is the last thing you want to do. I learned that some redemption can come from even the deepest of losses The victims of rape must carry their memories with them for the rest of their lives. They must not also carry the burden of silence and shame"—Nancy Venable Raine, *After Silence, Rape and My Journey Back.*

(Endnotes)

1 http://www.un.org/en/pseataskforce/docs/no_one_to_turn_under_reporting_of_child_sea_by_aid_workers.pdf

2 http://www.asafeworldforwomen.org/conflict/cp-africa/drcongo/725-women-in-dr-congo.html

3 http://www.policymic.com/articles/6618/the-balkan-war-legacy-rape-as-a-weapon-of-war

4 http://www.unicef.org/eapro/Child_Maltreatment.pdf

5 http://www.christianpost.com/news/the-invisible-war-female-soldiers-reveal-epidemic-of-sexual-assault-in-military-90042/#Q5wsvUO18pKQqk5O.99

6 http://www.refworld.org/docid/4f310baa2.html

7 http://www.worldwatchmonitor.org/research/2533678

SOS: Refugees

43.7 million people across our globe are refugees or forcibly displaced, primarily because of war or natural disasters. 26.4 million people are displaced inside their own countries. 80% are women and children, including large number of widows.

Immigrant, asylum seeker, refugee or displaced?

Although these terms are sometimes used interchangeably, an *immigrant* is a person who moves from one nation to settle in another one where they are not citizens. According to the United Nations, an *asylum seeker* or *refugee* is anyone "who, owing to a well-founded fear of being persecuted for reasons of race, religion, nationality, membership of a particular social group or political opinion, is outside the country of their nationality; and is unable to or—owing to such fear—unwilling to avail themselves of the protection of that country." The asylum seekers become refugees after their application to the government for asylum has been accepted.

All of the above people are "displaced," however, an *internally displaced person (IDP)* is someone who is forced to flee his or her home, but who remains within their country's borders. IDP's are often referred to as refugees as well, although they don't legally fall into that category. In 2011, the countries with the most number of IDPs were Colombia (3.8 million), Sudan (2.4 million), Democratic Republic of Congo (1.7 million), Somalia (1.4 million) and Iraq (1.3 million).[1] Although it is the hope of many displaced people to return to their homes, safely reclaiming their property often proves difficult if not impossible—especially for women.

Statelessness: Legal limbo

About 12 million other people in the world are "stateless," unable to claim a particular nationality and not recognized as citizens where they live. They may or may not be accepted as refugees. People can become stateless for a variety of reasons, including the break-up of nations such as the Soviet Union and Yugoslavia, or the creation of new countries. Migrants and ethnic groups like the Kurds and Roma people in some parts of Europe are other examples.

Stateless people have no legal protection or rights to participate in political processes, inadequate access to social services, poor employment prospects, little opportunity to own property or travel, and few protections against trafficking, harassment and violence. Statelessness has a disproportionate impact on women and children.[2]

Refugee camps

Tent cities and other emergency shelters for people who have been displaced, meant to be temporary, are sometimes pressed into service for years. Hundreds of thousands may be crowded into a single camp. Inadequate water and sanitation often leads to outbreaks of disease. Females may be totally without monthly sanitary supplies; even relief organizations seldom include them in aid packages, and there is insufficient water and soap to wash rags. A lack of privacy and basic protective measures like locks on doors also leads to harassment and violation of unaccompanied women. Those who have already lost homes and family members must endure further trauma.

Displaced women and children are increasingly targeted by armed elements for murder, abduction, forced military conscription and gender-based violence. In addition, women and children in conflict settings often face heightened health risks such as disruption of health services, facilitating the transmission of HIV and AIDS. Women frequently lack access to safe conditions for childbirth and emergency obstetric care.

Largest source and host countries

The latest available data from the United Nations Refugee Agency (UNHCR) in 2011 lists **Pakistan** as the country hosting the largest number of refugees: 1.7 million. **Afghanistan** retained the position as biggest source country with 2.7 million refugees, followed by **Iraq, Somalia, Sudan and Democratic Republic of the Congo. Syria** has since overtaken Iraq as the second biggest source country of refugees and may yet become the first (see below). 45% of refugees come from Asia, 27% from Africa, 15% from Europe and 8% from the Americas.

The journey of hope

Tragic headlines of refugees dying on their way to a new start are always hitting the news. 58 people from Afghanistan and Pakistan are drowned when their boat capsizes in the waters between Australia and Indonesia. The bodies of 54 Chinese men and four women are discovered in an airtight container at a UK port. Other travelers are frozen, suffocated, murdered or arrested; yet this does not deter the tens of thousands of men, women and children who continue to sell everything they own to pay people-smugglers. Over 80,000 people were convicted of illegally entering or re-entering the USA in 2012. Women and girls are at particular risk of dangerous and degrading encounters during their journey. The hazards are not over even when they reach processing or detention centers, especially if they are not accommodated separately from men.

Seeking asylum

Nearly half a million people sought asylum in the developed world in 2012, a 10-year high. The United States remained the most favored destination. Europe received the most asylum applications of all regions with Germany taking the lead, followed by France and Sweden. Women, especially those on their own or disabled or elderly, are not always aware of their rights when they apply. They may also be reluctant or fearful of recounting what they have suffered to male interviewers. Displaced people unable to provide documentation like birth certificates often have to wait for several years for a decision about their status. Meanwhile they can be denied basic services like health care and even schooling for their children. Qualifications that men and women have earned in their home countries, degrees and specialized training, may not be recognized. Single mothers who are not authorized to find employment in their host country and have inadequate means for food, rent and other requirements for their children are in a desperate situation. Other refugee women find that the stresses of their new lives lead to domestic abuse. Husbands may isolate them from opportunities that would help them gain fluency in the local language and integrate better with their communities. New arrivals could also face racism and discrimination.

Resentment of foreigners in many countries has led to a growing wave of anti-immigration legislation. This means millions of displaced people, instead of finding refuge, are driven into forced labor and sexual exploitation situations to stay alive.

A few refugee hotspots for women

* *Syria:* Conflict within this country has resulted in over two million refugees; numbers were still climbing in mid-2013. The great majority are women who are unused to going out to work and have no means of support. Some in desperation are offering themselves or their daughters in marriage. One woman arranging such marriages with Arab men says that most of them are between 50 and 80. "They ask for girls who have white skin and blue or green eyes. They want them very young, no older than 16."[3] Meanwhile, increasing reports have emerged of Syrian women being kidnapped, assaulted

or raped in refugee camps, particularly the Zaatari camp in Jordan where 100,000 have fled.

- ***Sudan and South Sudan:*** Prolonged civil war that eventually led to the division of Sudan into two countries in 2011 displaced some 5.5 million people. About 4 million are internally displaced and 1.5 million sought asylum in neighboring countries or overseas. Several thousand who tried to flee the Muslim North for South Sudan have ended up in crowded and insecure settlements near a contested section of the border between the two countries. Widows, pregnant and elderly women particularly struggle to walk the long distances necessary to find food and water, and they are sometimes attacked by local non-refugees. Adult women and adolescent girls have reported cases of rape or attempted rape, sexual abuse and harassment, although many instances of violence goes unreported due to fears of stigmatization. Victims who fall pregnant from such attacks are the ones who are blamed and ostracized.

- ***Greece:*** For hundreds of thousands of anxious men and women making their way from Eastern Europe, the Middle East, Asia and Africa, Athens is considered the gateway to the West. Many analysts believe there are between 1 to 1.3 million immigrants in the country, making up as much as 10 percent of the population. However, Amnesty International has protested new laws that allow detention of irregular migrants and asylum-seekers—often in appalling conditions—up to a year and a half, using grounds such as suspicion of carrying infectious diseases like HIV. Greece's dysfunctional system means that many destitute refugee women and children live on the streets.

- ***Britain:*** Approximately 30% of all applicants for asylum in the UK are women. Seven out of ten are unaccompanied by their husbands, although about half are caring for children. Among single women, almost 40% are mothers involuntarily separated from children. One refugee group estimates half of the women have been raped or sexually assaulted before reaching the UK; yet the charity Asylum Aid says the default setting for the UK Borders Agency is that women who claim to have been raped are lying.

Displaced women are often isolated and marginalized, particularly vulnerable to exploitation and domestic abuse. However, in many refugee communities around the world, violence to women often goes ignored by civil authorities. The inaction is justified as "respecting cultural differences." As long as male abusers are protected under the guise of political correctness, women have no place to turn.

Also see the section in this book titled "Vital Statistics: Rape as a weapon of war and religious extremism."

Action Steps

- Refugees probably live closer to you than you think. Find out where they are and offer practical help and friendship. You may even locate a refugee church. Resources about and for refugees and immigrants are available from some of the agencies listed under "Refugees" in Appendix 2 of this book. These can assist with cultural orientation, public benefits, child care and many other issues of concern to newcomers.

- Get your church or civic group to observe World Refugee Day. This was established by the United Nations on June 20th but it could become the focus of a World Refugee Sunday before or after that date. Perhaps you can include a fundraiser for a particular mission project aimed at helping refugees.

"Lord, you know the hopes of humble people. Surely you will hear their cries and comfort their hearts by helping them. You will be with the orphans and all who are oppressed, so that mere earthly man will terrify them no longer."
Psalm 10:17,18; The Living Bible

(Endnotes)
1   http://www.unhcr.org.uk/about-us/key-facts-and-figures.html
2   http://www.refintl.org/what-we-do/statelessness
3   http://www.bbc.co.uk/news/world-middle-east-22473573

SOS: Religious Slaves

Although it is called religious or ritual servitude, the reality is that this is one of the most heinous forms of child slavery today.

INDIA and NEPAL

"It's hard for us to understand the depths of the exploitation these women suffer, the brokenness of their spirits. A devadasi *is a* dalit *[untouchable], so she's low on the social scale anyway. But when she's a* devadasi *she's worth nothing: the lowest of the low."*
—Dr. B. D'Souza, Indian pediatrician

The practice was legally abolished over 150 years ago, yet poor parents in southern India and Nepal continue to give away daughters as young as five years old in "marriage" ceremonies to Hindu gods or temples. Besides ridding themselves of unwanted girls, families hope their offering will appease the deity and bring them favor. In the past such girls, sometimes called *devadasis* or *jogini*, served as sacred temple slaves or dancers. Once they reached puberty they were expected to provide sexual services to any males who were their social superior. Missionary Amy Carmichael dedicated her life to the rescue and care of hundreds of these children.

Today's temple slaves are exploited until the priests tire of them, then sold to the highest bidder as child concubines. Eventually the girls (and any children they conceive) are turned out on the streets to survive any way they can. Still "married to the gods," they are not allowed to marry anyone else. Most are forced into brothels, their distinctive bangles and pendant necklaces declaring their original status as temple prostitutes.

Today there are an estimated 70,000 *devadasis* in the state of Karnataka alone and 250,000 in all of India. However, women's groups are campaigning against it and some Christian organizations are offering alternative lifestyles to freed girls.[1]

WEST AFRICA

Thousands of West African girls as young as four years old have also been offered to the gods, as atonement for some offence committed by a relative. *"Trokosi,"* which literally means *"slave wives of the gods,"* are part of a 300-year tradition in the Upper Volta region that encompasses Ghana, Nigeria, Benin and Togo. Until the 18th Century, fetish priests accepted livestock as offerings by families who were fearful of retribution by the gods. But then the priests decided a young virgin would be more useful for domestic and sexual purposes.

A slave's term of service is supposed to last from three to five years, depending on the nature of the sin that is being atoned for. However, most families of *trokosi* cannot afford the very high redemption price required to buy their daughters back. They also live in real fear of the gods' displeasure. If a priest dies, the woman becomes the property of his successor. But if the girl dies without her family redeeming her, they must replace her with another virgin. They must also replace her if she runs away. The cycle can continue for generations.

Trokosi slaves live in inhuman conditions: frequently raped and beaten, given only rags to wear and forced to beg for food, they receive no education or medical attention and work long hours in the priest's fields. They often suffer from ill health. Babies born to the girls must also become slaves to the priest, although he takes no responsibility for their care and she must provide for them. Those who resist are beaten into submission.[2]

Through the efforts of non-government organizations many shrines have now stopped the practice of *trokosi* and 2,900 women have been freed and rehabilitated. In 1998 Ghana passed a law banning the practice. However, thousands of girls still remain in slavery—some estimate up to 35,000 in the four countries. The law is hard to enforce as many people insist that it is a part of their culture and fear the power of the gods—and the priests.

Note: Major source for material in this section is the Anti-Slavery Society.

Action Steps

- Support the work of Every Child Ministries and International Needs, both of which help to liberate and rehabilitate *trokosi* girls, and work towards the abolition of the system. Perhaps you, your church or other group could raise funds that will allow them to purchase back the lives of enslaved children.

- The Dalit Freedom Network is one of only a handful of non-government agencies that is working among India's *devadasis*. It also advocates for the plight of dalit women and children and provides education and health care. See Appendix 2 for websites.

"We have escaped like a bird out of the fowler's snare; the snare has been broken, and we have escaped." Psalm 124:7

SOS: Trafficking of Girls & Women

Illegal trade in human beings is the top human rights issue of the 21st Century. It is one of the world's fastest-growing and lucrative businesses, earning about $32 billion per year, or $87 million every day. An estimated 27 million adults and 13 million children on this planet are victims of human trafficking. Every nation is involved.

- The majority of people who are imported and exported within or over borders are used in forced labor or sex. Eighty percent are female. Pregnant women are not exempt; in fact they are sometimes targeted, their babies sold on the black market when they are born.

- Fifty to sixty percent of those who are trafficked *are babies and children.* 1.2 million children (two-thirds of them girls) fall victim every year. The huge demand for adopted infants in many countries provides a ready market. About half of older children are used for sex, the rest for cheap forced labor or begging. Some girls are abducted, others sold by destitute parents; the younger the child is, the more traffickers receive. Fear of AIDS is driving the market for younger sexual partners. The average life span of a child caught in the sex slave trade is two years. They are either beaten to death, contract HIV and AIDS or bacterial meningitis, or overdose on drugs forced on them.[1]

- Today's slaves are cheaper than they have ever been in history. Unemployment, poverty, displacement and gender discrimination have all contributed to a limitless supply of vulnerable workers who are easily enslaved by the greedy. And unlike drugs, a person can be sold again and again.

- The trafficking network includes recruiters (those who win and and abuse their victims' trust); smugglers or transporters; people who provide counterfeit IDs and travel documents; those who watch the victims so they don't escape; the clients (owners and managers of nightclubs, brothels and other destination employers); and those who deliver or launder the money involved.

- In about 43 percent of cases, recruiters know the victims. Many young women are lured to another country by false promises of legitimate work or by "loverboys" who groom girls into relationships. Sex traffickers can earn 20 times what they pay for a girl. They often condition their victims themselves using starvation, drugs, violence, humiliation and rape, also teach them how to perform acts of sex.

- *Organ harvesting*, while not as prevalent as labor or sex trafficking, is quite real. The World Health Organization estimates that as many as 7,000 kidneys are illegally obtained by traffickers every year as demand outstrips the supply of organs legally available for transplant. The going price for kidneys is $62,000 while livers can bring twice that amount, and hearts and lungs even more.[2] In some countries, homeless people have been targeted for forcible removal of organs and left for dead. In April 2013, an EU-led court sentenced five doctors for illegal removal and transplant of kidneys. The donors were recruited from poor Eastern European and Central Asian countries who were promised about 15,000 Euros ($19,540) for their organs.[3] The first case of an individual (female) being trafficked to Britain in order to have their organs harvested was uncovered in 2012. According to Doctors Against Forced Organ Harvesting, China has harvested the organs of executed prisoners for almost 30 years. However, reports suggest that organs have also been removed from living prisoners of conscience, and transplanted for profit.[4]

- Sex trafficking has played a major role in the worldwide spread of HIV and AIDS. Since girls forced into prostitution routinely receive more money for sex without condoms, this is the practice preferred by most of their "owners."

The **"Convention on the Elimination of All Forms of Discrimination Against Women,"** often described as an international bill of rights for women, was adopted back in 1979 by the UN's General Assembly. Trafficking in women was defined to include "sexual slavery, generally and by the military, the deception of migrant women, and 'mail order' and false marriages." The Convention urged countries to "take all appropriate measures, including legislation, to suppress all forms of traffic in women and exploitation or prostitution of women." All nations that ratified this declaration made themselves legally bound to enforce it. The seven UN member states that have not ratified or acceded to the convention are Iran, Palau, Somalia, South Sudan, Sudan, Tonga and the United States. The United States and Palau have signed it, but not yet ratified it.

At least 60 countries have passed tough new anti-trafficking legislation in the last decade. In spite of these measures, trafficking continues to increase.

EUROPE

A 2012 study by the International Labour Organization indicated that 880,000 people in the European Union are in forced labor, including sexual exploitation. Many are underage. A large portion come from Central and Eastern Europe. The EU commission said the economic crisis is leading to the rising number of people being trafficked for sex, hard labor and organ donation. Lack of border controls between EU countries has facilitated trafficking, and legalized prostitution in many places also creates opportunities for crime. Twenty-one member states have failed to implement an anti-trafficking law.[5]

- *Moldova:* The women of Europe's poorest country are its biggest export. Since 1991, over 450,000 girls have gone missing from this small post-Soviet nation of just four million people.

- *Bulgaria:* Along with Romania, the EU's two poorest countries also fuel the trafficking industry. Those of ethnic Roma (gypsy) origin are most vulnerable. Although exact numbers are impossible because of underground operations, approximately 10,000 Bulgarian women are thought to be current victims of international trafficking operations in various countries.

- One-third of victims in *Romania* are children. Homeless children in particular have increasingly been trafficked under false pretenses and forced into prostitution in Spain, Greece, Germany and Holland. The birth of thousands of children in Romania and many other countries are not registered, so they can just "disappear."

- *Albania:* Over 8,000 Albanian girls have been sent into Italy's sex trade, more than 30% of them under 18 years. Teenage girls are kidnapped almost daily from village streets, discos, even schools. Children are exploited for forced begging, petty crimes and other jobs in many parts of Europe.

- **Austria's** media in 2013 reported plans by an Austrian businessman to open Europe's largest brothel, a 14.2 million Euro FunMotel, at a secret location near the Czech border. The owner expects to offer 1,000 visitors a day females at "affordable prices." A 2010 study by the European Network for HIV/STI Prevention and Health Promotion among Migrant Sex Workers showed 78 percent of sex workers in Austria are not Austrian nationals.[6]

- *Italy:* Trafficking women and girls for prostitution and forced labor in Italy is a growing problem. Girls are most commonly transported from Albania, Nigeria, the former Soviet Union and Eastern Europe.

- **Germany:** The police pick up or are contacted by some 600 to 800 young women every year who are victims of human traffickers. Estimates suggest that at least 10,000 women, mostly from Eastern and Central Europe, live as forced prostitutes out of three to four hundred thousand full and part-time sex workers. A very small number of them manage to escape and run away.[7] Yet women from abroad who escape prostitution are considered "illegal immigrants" in Germany and only allowed to remain during the criminal proceedings when they testify against the perpetrators. Although they take a great personal risk by making a statement they are deported when the case is closed, generally without financial compensation. Prostitution is legal and so are brothels, although many are illegally registered as wellness clubs.

- **Greece:** Increasingly being used as both a destination and transit point for trafficking, with 16,000 to 20,000 women in the country at any one time. An academic observer estimated that approximately 40,000 women, most between the ages of 12 and 25, are trafficked to Greece each year for prostitution. Seventy-five percent of girls are deceived into thinking they will be given other types of employment.

- **Netherlands:** The number of reported victims of trafficking has almost trebled in the last 10 years. 25,000 women, many from poor countries, work as prostitutes, and an expert from NGO Equality Now says that around 80 to 90 percent of women are foreigners.[8] Many African girls brought here are re-sold to other European countries.

- **Ukraine:** Approximately 117,000 Ukrainians have been forced into servitude through the years, the majority of them women and children. Most women fall victim through phony job offers and are later forced into prostitution. Orphans are made vulnerable by the lack of protection and oversight when they leave state institutions.[9]

- **United Kingdom:** A study by the Center for Social Justice in 2013 identified 1,000 cases of trafficking but cautioned that official figures remain "a pale reflection of the true size of the problem." The report uncovered a "shocking underworld" and bemoaned the fact that social workers were "not equipped" to identify victims of modern slavery. Police too, often fell short of providing critical protection.

ASIA

Southeast Asia is one of the world's largest exporters of sex slaves to brothels in Japan, China, Australia, Europe and the United States. The owner of a brothel in Southeast Asia can buy a woman or child for as little as $50.[10]

- **Thailand:** This country continues to be one of the top hubs of human trafficking. The Coalition Against Trafficking in Women has estimated that one million women and children of various nationalities have been trafficked into Thailand, with the highest numbers imported for prostitution from **Burma (Myanmar)**. At least 50,000 Burmese girls and women are working in Thailand as prostitutes at any one time. Tens of thousands of girls are also transported from **Southern China, Cambodia, Laos, Vietnam, Uzbekistan** and **Russia.**

Internal trafficking is also big in Thailand, with parents sending daughters into Bangkok's sex trade to earn money for the family. A trafficker in the country typically pays $25 to "rent" a child beggar.* Another 3,000 Thai women and children are annually sent to nearby *Cambodia* for prostitution, and to *China* for domestic work. A large number of Thai women—up to 70,000—endure slave-like conditions in the Japanese sex industry.

- **Nepal:** An estimated 12,000 to 15,000 girls between the ages of 6 and 16 are taken over the border to India every year. Most are either kidnapped by traffickers or sold by destitute parents for domestic or factory labor; or, if they are teenagers, for sex work. Traffickers sell girls or women to city brokers for around $1000, who in turn sell them on to brothels. When girls contract AIDS, as a high number do, they are discarded. So are any HIV-positive babies.

- **China:** This is a major source, transit and destination country for trafficking. As many as 90 percent of the 600,000 Chinese who annually seek work overseas go through illegal channels, using international syndicates and local gangs. The number of Chinese women forced into prostitution overseas is rising and up to 20,000 children are annually kidnapped for illegal adoption.[11] In addition, a shortage of females due to China's "one child" policy has led to the trafficking of at least 250,000 women and children within China.

SOUTH ASIA

- **Bangladesh:** Human rights monitors estimate that more than 20,000 women and children are annually trafficked from this country for the purpose of forced prostitution. In 2013, International Christian Concern reported the rescue of more than 140 children from Islamic training centers (madrassas) in the previous nine months. A majority of internally trafficked children like these are targeted because of their Christian faith. Nearly half of those rescued were female; they said they had been used for forced labor in Muslim homes and for sex slavery.[12]

- **Pakistan:** According to a report by the Asian Human Rights Commission, a possible 20,000 children suffering from microcephaly are sent into servitude as forced beggars. Microcephaly is a neurological development disorder that causes children to have small heads. Thousands of Pakistani children as young as four were also trafficked into the United Arab Emirates and other Gulf countries to work as camel jockeys. This abusive practice was banned in 2002 but not enforced until 2005.[13]

MIDDLE EAST

The International Labour Organization reported in 2013 that as many as 600,000 migrant workers may be trapped into forced labor in the Middle East. Many live in appalling conditions; raped, abused or kept prisoner.[14]

Lebanon: Women from Ethiopia, the former USSR, and up to 170,000 Sri Lankans have gone to Lebanon expecting to work as domestics; instead they have reported being forced into slave labor and sexually exploited.

Turkey: A top destination for victims of trafficking, especially women from the former Soviet Union.

Iraq: Virgin teenage girls in Iraq are reported to be sold to human traffickers for $5,000, double the price of non-virgins. The girls are trafficked to Northern Iraq, Syria and the United Arab Emirates.*

Saudi Arabia: An estimated 1,000 to 1,500 children from India and neighboring countries are smuggled into Saudi Arabia every year to beg for their employers during the Haj season. They are likely to face beatings and are sometimes even mutilated to try to improve the chances of earning more money. Only a small number ever return home.

AFRICA

South Africa: Major transit point between the developing world and Europe, USA and Canada. Trafficking of women and children into forced prostitution here has now become the third largest source of profits for organized crime, after drugs and guns. Girls are commonly taken from malls, bus stops and taxi ranks and drugged. While they are drugged they are raped and photos are taken which are used to threaten and control them. Clothes and shoes are taken away, so they don't escape. South Africa has some 30,000 child prostitutes.

Mozambique: According to UNICEF, every year around 1,000 Mozambican women and children are sold to brothels in South Africa and other countries. Traffickers can buy a girl for as little as $2 up to $1000.*

Ghana: The human trafficking market in Ghana allows a child to be purchased from parents for $50. The trafficker can then either sell or lease out that child for up to $300, thus making $250 per year in profit.*

Nigeria: UNESCO ranks human trafficking as the third most common crime in Nigeria, after fraud and drug trafficking. Teenage mothers are sometimes forced to hand their newborns over to traffickers, who can sell them into illegal adoptions for up to $6,400 each, depending on the sex. Although buying or selling babies can carry a 14-year jail sentence, few traffickers are ever caught.[15] Transporting young Nigerian women to other countries is also a major business. Girls are often coerced by threats to their families and voodoo rituals. The United Nations estimates that between 8,000 to 10,000 women are trafficked into the prostitution industry *in Italy alone* every year. They are then forced to repay their pimps between $40,000 to $78,000.[16]

LATIN AMERICA

- ***Brazil:*** This country's improving economy has attracted rising numbers of immigrants from Bangladesh, Haiti and Africa, encouraging gangs that specialize in people smuggling. Once in Brazil, immigrants are then exploited and forced to pay the smugglers $10,000. An average of 1,000 Brazilians each year are transported abroad and subjected mainly to sexual exploitation and slave labor.

- ***Colombia:*** Interpol estimates 35,000 females are trafficked out of Colombia every year, with estimated profits of $500 million. The average age of the trafficked victim is 14.[17]

- **Mexico:** Listed by the United Nations as the number one source for the supply of young children to North America. The majority are sent to international pedophile organizations. Most of the children over 12 end up as prostitutes.

CARIBBEAN

- **Dominican Republic:** Has the highest rate of trafficking in the Caribbean. Dominican women and children are reportedly subjected to forced prostitution in their own country and throughout the Caribbean, Europe, South America and the United States. Smuggling rings have sent more than 50,000 into the overseas sex trade. Girls are often lured into marriages under false pretences, and then sold into prostitution by so-called "husbands."

- **Haiti:** Since Haiti's 2010 earthquake, an extensive network has developed. An estimated 200,000 to 300,000 victims are internally trafficked, while international trafficking numbers are in the low thousands. Smugglers charge up to $5000 per person for (false promises of) work or education packages. Over 3,000 Haitians were sold in South America in 2011.[18]

NORTH AMERICA

Canada: An estimated 300,000 people are victims of human trafficking in Canada: 150,000 people are brought into the country from overseas, and the same number are trafficked domestically around the country.* Each week this country receives about twelve 16 to 30 year-old Asian girls and women on visitor's permits. They are then sold to brothel owners in Markham, Scarborough, Toronto and Los Angeles, and forced into $40,000 debt bondage. Vietnamese and Chinese mafia are expanding operations in Toronto brothels, trafficking women from Southeast Asia. Within Canada, sex trafficking of females is high among First Nation or Aboriginal girls.

A pimp will pay a trafficker about 5,000 Canadian dollars to buy one girl, and earn up to $280,000 from her in one year. *

USA: Human trafficking has been reported in all 50 states, most commonly in New York, California and Florida. The FBI estimates that up to 18,000 women and children a year are brought across borders, primarily for the sex industry but also to make money for their "owners" as maids, trinket peddlars on subways and buses, sweatshop or agricultural workers and beggars. Most children are between 12 and 14 years old when they enter America's commercial sex industry. In 2008, the U.S.

Border Patrol apprehended roughly 8,000 unaccompanied minors at the border. By 2012, that number ballooned to nearly 25,000.[19]

The United States is the major destination country for young children kidnapped and trafficked for adoption by childless couples, unwilling to wait for a child through legitimate adoption procedures and agencies. The largest source country is Mexico. Mexican children over 12 years of age are also kidnapped and trafficked to the U.S. for child prostitution.

Chinese women are being sold into the States for brothels in New York and North Carolina, then forced to work off $40,000 in debt bondage. Some trafficked women are made to pay for their transport by having sex with up to 500 men.

Action Steps:

Consider hosting a "Freedom Sunday" in your church that promotes awareness of the trafficking issue. See the "Not for Sale" website and other organization websites listed under "Traffic in Women and Girls" in Appendix 2.

How equipped is your city or country to recognize and deal with victims of human slavery? Find out what shelter facilities and support workers, if any, are available. In most places there is a great deficiency of safe accommodation and counselling of seriously traumatized girls and women, particularly those who are foreign-born. The Salvation Army is one agency that has made care of survivors a priority. Perhaps you can volunteer. Encourage politicians to introduce more measures to help, and get others to lobby with you.

"But this is a people plundered and looted, all of them trapped in pits or hidden away in prisons. They have become plunder with no one to rescue them." Isaiah 42:22

*Information source: Havoscope, Global Black Market Information, at havoscope.com

(Endnotes)
1 http://www.mannafreedom.com/get-informed-about-human-trafficking/what-is-human-trafficking/
2 http://fightslaverynow.wordpress.com/why-fight-there-are-27-million-reasons/otherformsoftrafficking/organ-removal/
3 http://www.rawstory.com/rs/2013/04/29/five-doctors-jailed-in-kosovo-for-illegal-organ-harvesting-and-transplants/
4 http://www.dafoh.org/unethical-organ-harvesting/forced-organ-harvesting-in-china/
5 http://euobserver.com/social/119800
6 http://www.praguepost.com/news/16280-out-in-the-open.html

7 http://www.dw.de/germany-lags-behind-in-protection-of-forced-prostitutes/a-16837388

8 http://www.praguepost.com/news/16280-out-in-the-open.html

9 http://www.mannafreedom.com/get-informed-about-human-trafficking/what-is-human-trafficking

10 http://www.mannafreedom.com/get-informed-about-human-trafficking/what-is-human-trafficking/

11 http://www.humantrafficking.org/countries/china

12 http://www.persecution.org/2013/05/05/young-christian-girls-trafficked-into-forced-labor-and-sex-slavery/

13 http://www.soschildrensvillages.ca/news/news/child-charity-news/pages/child-trafficking-pakistan-715.aspx

14 http://edition.cnn.com/2013/04/09/world/meast/mideast-migrant-workers

15 http://www.guardian.co.uk/law/2011/jun/02/nigeria-baby-farm-raided-human-trafficking

16 http://www.voanews.com/content/most-trafficked-into-italys-sex-trade-nigerians-150206105/370025.html

17 http://www.orphanhopeintl.org/facts-statistics/

18 http://www.alterpresse.org/spip.php?article13616#.UZ35pNhTEow

19 http://www.aljazeera.com/indepth/opinion/2013/04/201342387040405.html

SOS: Widows

When a woman is widowed she becomes a member of one of the world's largest, most marginalized and invisible of people groups. Women who are already traumatized become society's victims.

Of the world's 245 million widows, 115 million live in extreme poverty and 81 million have been abused, simply because they are widows. More than 1.5 million of their children will die before the age of five.[1]

AFRICA

Millions of widows in sub-Saharan Africa are robbed, beaten, raped, and evicted from their homes—often by their own in-laws—because women are considered unworthy of equal property rights. Unlawful treatment is even more common when a husband dies of AIDS.

▶**Cameroon:** In the Highlands, when a man dies, society quickly accuses the wife of witchcraft. She is forced to shave her head and wear only rags for seven weeks. She cannot bathe or cook. For the next year she may not earn money or act as the head of the household. Ill treatment of the widow is considered a punishment, a test of fidelity and a cleansing exercise. For the widower, however, there are few consequences. He may return to work immediately and soon remarry.

▶**Ghana** has six "witch camps," each with up to 1,000 women who have fled there to avoid beatings, torture or death after being named as witches. A BBC news story in September 2012 reported that the majority of the women in these camps are elderly and perhaps three-fourths are widows, suggesting that the accusations are made in order to take control of the widows' property. Conditions in the camps are basic, without running water or electricity, and they offer little means of survival.

▶**Mali:** A new family law in 2012 reduced the rights of Mali's widows. Before this they were automatically allowed to keep their children. Now a family council decides who keeps them.

▶**Zimbabwe:** It is common for widows in rural areas to be accused of causing the death of their husbands, also of bewitching people and inflicting them with AIDS. Such women and their children are usually evicted from their homes and disinherited. Widows are the poorest and most stigmatized group in society.

▶**Nigerian** widows are also often blamed for murdering their husbands, unless they can show proof of their innocence. Employment opportunities are scarce and most live in destitution.

▶**In Swaziland**, women have only limited rights to own land, enter into contractual agreements and function independently of their fathers and husbands. When their men die, Swazi women are left without land, money or skills to earn a living.

▶**Zambia:**[2] As in many other areas, widows suffer discrimination and injustice and are often deprived of an inheritance. Required acts of mourning may include being:

- Forced to crawl around the funeral house or grave of their deceased husbands
- Slapped and starved
- Prevented from bathing or changing their clothing for days, weeks or a month
- Kept under a blanket until the burial
- Insulted and shouted at with obscenities
- Accused of having killed their husband, and submitted to trial by ordeal
- Stripped half-naked
- Deprived of some or all of their property
- Sexually "cleansed" (see below); for example, by insisting they have sex with a relative of their deceased husband
- Denied custody of their children, even small babies
- Forced to live with in-laws
- Denied freedom of movement for months or even years; a virtual house arrest

In some areas of Africa, widows are forced to undergo sexual rituals in order to keep their property. *"Wife inheritance"* entitles a male relative of the dead husband to take over the widow as his wife, often in a polygamous family. *"Ritual cleansing"* usually involves sex with a social outcast like the village drunk, who is paid by the dead husband's family. This is supposed to cleanse the woman of her husband's evil spirits. Not only is this practice humiliating and degrading but dangerous, often leading to the spread of AIDS. Women who fight back are routinely beaten, raped, or ostracized. Since the hundreds of thousands of "cleansers" at work across Africa are obviously spreading disease, some though not all villages have discontinued this practice.[3]

ASIA

▶**Nepal:** The most severe form of widow abuse is labelling her a *bokshi* (witch), and holding her responsible for the death of her husband. Such women may be stoned, beaten or burned to death. Other widows—

especially in non-urban parts of Nepal[4]—are generally treated as outcasts, and physically abused by the authorities in their communities. In some areas widows are forced to shave their heads and wear white clothes. In most parts they are restricted to eating vegetarian food with limits on spices, etc. Widows have to cook for themselves and cannot eat food touched by others.

▶**India: Widow Burning**

The Hindu tradition of *sati* or suttee used to dictate that widows threw themselves (or were pushed) onto the funeral pyres of their husbands. This was outlawed in 1829 after the cruel deaths of thousands of women. However, the practice continued for many years afterwards and still takes place very occasionally.[5]

After the legal ban on suttee, widows were often subjected to a ceremony that formally degraded them. Their heads were shaved and they were forbidden the use of personal ornaments. Even today, India's *estimated 40 million* widows—both Hindu and Muslim—are commonly blamed, shamed and robbed of property rights. Many flee their homes to escape abusive in-laws. In tribal communities, widows may be accused of being a witch, and killed. Hindu widows who remarry are frowned upon; the higher the caste or social position, the more their restrictions. In some castes *leviratic* marriage is practised: the widow is taken on by a brother. The daughters of widows probably face an even bleaker future. With no one to provide a dowry they are married off to almost anyone who will take them, usually older men.[6]

Left Behind

In 2001, after the huge Hindu Kumbh Mela festival in Allahabad that drew millions of worshippers from all over India, families left behind 10,000 elderly widowed mothers and other unwanted relatives. These poor and infirm women survived as best they could from one day to the next, hoping someone would return for them. Unwanted people were again abandoned after the 2013 Kumbh Mela and an estimated 10,000 live in destitution in the sacred cities of Allahabad and Varanasi.[7] Another 15,000 ostracised Hindu widows wait for death in the sacred city of Vrindaven in central India, believing that dying there will free them from the endless cycle of reincarnation.[8]

▶**Sri Lanka:** Years of internal fighting in this country have left many thousands of widows. Wives of men who died in the armed forces are only entitled to benefits if they do not marry. But women without men in this culture are considered abnormal, and they are vulnerable to sexual and economic exploitation. Widows also fear that if they remarry, the children by their first husbands will be mistreated.

MIDDLE EAST

▶**Afghanistan:** With an estimated two million war widows, Afghanistan has been called the widows' capital of the world. Up to 50,000 in Kabul alone struggle each day to feed and protect their children. Most have had little education and have never worked outside their homes. To other family members, a widow is a liability.[9]

▶**Iraq:** Over two million of this country's women are widows—most of their husbands taken by war. Some accept "temporary marriages" in order to survive, although there is great shame and social stigma attached. [See also "Vital Statistics: Brides at Risk"]

ACTION STEPS

International Widows Day, observed on the 23rd of June every year, was created by the UN General Assembly in 2010 to highlight violations of the rights of widowed women with a view to ensuring their protection under national and international law, empowering them and restoring their human dignity. Why not raise the profile of these suffering women by recognizing International Widows Day? Perhaps your church or other women's group can raise funds to support a mission project that involves widow relief.

Religion that God our Father accepts as pure and faultless is this: to look after orphans and widows in their distress.... James 1:27

(Endnotes)

1 http://appealforwidows.org/

2 http://allafrica.com/stories/201109020279.html; http://www.thebelievers.org/widows. html

3 http://www.genderacrossborders.com/2011/10/28/scrape-her-head-and-lay-her-bare-widowhood-practices-and-culture/;   http://www.bnltimes.com/index.php/sunday-times/ headlines/national/12079-sex-cleanser-slept-with-104-widows

4 http://asiafoundation.org/in-asia/2012/08/08/legislating-against-witchcraft-accusations-in-nepal/

5 http://www.refworld.org/cgi-bin/texis/vtx/rwmain?page=country&category=&publish er=RDCI&type=&coi=IND&rid=&docid=4b17a0cdf&skip=0

6 Ibid.

7 http://articles.latimes.com/2012/oct/16/world/la-fg-india-widows-20121016

8 http://www.rawa.org/temp/runews/2007/05/17/forgotten-women-turn-kabul-into-widows-capital.html

9 http://english.cntv.cn/program/asiatoday/20120924/107612.shtml

SOS: Women and the AIDS Pandemic*

In 2012, UNAIDS named the human immunodeficiency virus (HIV) the leading cause of death in women of reproductive age globally. 7,400 people become infected with HIV every day, and women account for nearly half the approximately *34 million people living with the virus.* In 2011 an estimated 1.2 million women and girls were newly infected. The proportion of AIDS diagnoses reported among women has more than tripled since 1985. The vast majority contract the disease through sexual intercourse with men.

The "Virgin Cure"

Back in 18th Century Europe, men with syphilis paid to have sexual relations with little girls because they believed a virgin could cure them. Today many men in Africa and Asia believe that intercourse with a virgin can cure the AIDS virus. This has led to a tragic increase of infection among young girls.

Widow Inheritance and Cleansing

In some African countries it has long been a tradition for women whose husbands have died to be "inherited" by their brothers or other close relatives. In many instances, widows must be "cleansed" by having sex with a relative before she is inherited. This centuries-old ritual in Zambia, Kenya, Malawi, Uganda, Tanzania, Ghana, Senegal, Angola, Ivory Coast, Congo and Nigeria is believed necessary to set free the spirit of the deceased husband. Not to do so would put both the widow and the whole village at risk. Unsurprisingly, these traditions have fueled the rapid spread of HIV and AIDS: husbands have transmitted HIV to their wives before dying, and widows have been forced to have sexual relations with HIV-infected relatives.

THE FACTS

- Physiologically, women are up to four times more vulnerable to HIV infection than men. Every minute around the world, a young woman is newly infected with HIV. Girls aged 15-24 are the most vulnerable, and young women with sexual partners 10 or more years older are two to four times more likely to be infected than young women with partners of the same age or one year older.

- Many women with HIV are not receiving regular care.

- Transmission from men to women is twice as likely as from women to men. The risk is especially high in the case of unwilling sex with an infected partner, since condom use is unlikely. Violence such as forced prostitution, incest and rape—including marital rape—all put women and girls at risk of contracting HIV. A South African report suggests that one in seven cases of young women acquiring HIV could have been prevented had they not been subjected to intimate partner violence.

- In some societies it is commonly believed that only "bad" females have any knowledge of sex before they marry. The truth is that lack of information contributes greatly to a girl's vulnerability and can ultimately prove fatal. Globally, less than 30% of young women have correct and comprehensive knowledge about HIV.

- Maternal mortality worldwide would be 20% lower in the absence of HIV.

- About 17.3 million children worldwide suffer as "AIDS orphans" through the death of at least one parent. In Rwanda, an estimated 45,000 households are headed by children because of the AIDS-related deaths of parents. Ninety percent of these heads of households are girls.

- The enormous social stigma of being HIV-infected leads many women to risk mother-to-child transmission of the virus by breastfeeding, since not to breastfeed infants would alert communities to their HIV status. Globally, only 57% of infected pregnant women engage in Prevention of Mother-to-Child Transmission (PMTCT) programs.

- HIV-positive people are far more vulnerable to developing illnesses like tuberculosis and severe forms of malaria because their weak immune systems simply cannot respond to the disease effectively.

- Globally, 46 percent of people who need anti-retroviral treatment don't get it.

- Despite the increase and availability of HIV testing, *about one in five people who are infected with HIV are unaware that they carry it.* People diagnosed late are 10 times more likely to die within a year of testing positive.

"This epidemic unfortunately remains an epidemic of women."
Michel Sidibé, Executive Director of UNAIDS

GLOBAL SNAPSHOTS:

- **Sub-Saharan Africa** remains the epicenter of the AIDS pandemic, with one in every 20 adults infected by HIV. 58% of all HIV-positive adults are women. Teenage girls are as much as eight times more likely to contract AIDS than boys.

- **Swaziland**, followed by **Botswana and Lesotho**, currently has the highest HIV prevalence rate in the world at 26%, 25% and 24%. **South Africa** comes fourth with just under 18% or 5.6 million people living with HIV and AIDS. Almost a third of South African deaths in 2011 were AIDS-related. Although the death rate is slowing, there are increasing numbers of AIDS orphans.

- After sub-Saharan Africa, the regions most heavily affected are **Eastern Europe and Central Asia.** AIDS-related deaths have increased by 21 percent. Drug injection is a major means of transmission, probably because only five percent of drug injectors use sterile equipment. Only 25% of those eligible for treatment receive it. HIV prevalence is twice as high among young women than young men in these regions.

- In **Latin America** the epidemic has seen a slight decrease, but there is only 56% of PMTCT coverage, and only 68% of infected people receive antiretroviral treatment. The **Caribbean** has had a 42% decline in new infections.

- **North America:** There's been an increase in the number of people living with HIV and AIDS. In the **United States**, 80% of HIV incidence is among African American and Hispanic women. Heterosexual sex is the dominant means of transmission. New York has by far the greatest number of females living with HIV, followed by Florida, Texas, California and New Jersey. More than 8 in 10 women have been diagnosed, but only 70% have been linked to care. In **Canada**, about one in four people are unaware they are HIV-positive. Half of all positive diagnoses in females in recent years were made when they were under 20 years old. [AVERT]

- The number of new infections in the **Middle East and North Africa** has increased by over 35% since 2001, and deaths increased by 17%. The majority of women are infected by their husbands or partners who engage in high-risk behaviour and are mostly unaware of their status. Only 7% of HIV-infected pregnant women receive PMTCT. Early marriage in this region forces young girls to have sex when their bodies are not fully developed. This makes them vulnerable to tearing and abrasions that can lead to HIV infection. In **Senegal**, men who were surveyed believed that female genital mutilation is advantageous as it reduces women's desire and helps them resist men. The truth is that this practice increases women's risk of contracting HIV and AIDS. [See the section on "Vital Statistics - Female Genital Mutilation"]

• **Western Europe: Great Britain** had more new diagnoses of HIV than any other country in 2011; however, **France** and **Spain** both have around double the prevalence of HIV in the population. One in 25 Africans in the UK are HIV-positive: 40 times the white population. 91 percent of transmission is through heterosexual sex but 4.5 percent is mother-to-child. Around one in four people in Britain don't know they have the virus. [Terrence Higgins Trust]

Stepping Up the Suffering

In too many areas HIV-positive women are subject to *physical and emotional abuse, accusations of infidelity, discrimination, rejection and even, sometimes, murder* when their positive status is revealed. In some places women are even held responsible for the AIDS-related deaths of their husbands.

Nearly four in 10 countries worldwide still lack any specific legal provisions to prevent or address HIV-related discrimination. In Nigeria, for instance, one in five people living with HIV are denied health services. Twenty countries have laws that allow them to deport individuals who are discovered living with HIV. Forty-four countries have some kinds of restrictions on travelers with the virus, and five completely bar entry.

Forced sterilization of HIV-positive women in Namibia came to light in 2007 and there is evidence of at least 15 sterilizations since 2008. Similar stories have been documented in Zambia and in the Democratic Republic of Congo.

The Good News

Although national epidemics continue to expand in many places, 25 countries have seen a 50% or more drop in new infections since 2001.

In 2011, 57% of pregnant women living with HIV in low- and middle-income countries received effective drug regimens to prevent mother-to-child transmission. Half of all reductions in new infections in the last two years have been among newborn babies.

Sub-Saharan Africa has reduced AIDS-related deaths by one-third in the last six years and more people are receiving treatment, including 59% of pregnant women living with HIV. Over eight million people are now taking antiretroviral drugs. Access has improved since the cost has dropped dramatically from $10,000 per person in 2000 to less than $100 per person for the least expensive WHO-recommended regimen. However, seven million people who need medicines still lack access.

81 countries increased their domestic investments for AIDS research and treatment by more than 50% between 2006 and 2011. By 2015, the estimated annual need will be $22 to 24 billion.

*Sources most used: UNAIDS Fact Sheet and Global Reports; Kaiser Family Foundation

Action Steps

World AIDS Day on December 1st every year is an opportunity to unite in the fight against this devastating disease. Help others to understand the issues by making books and leaflets available or ask a person who is HIV positive to share with your group. Do a fundraiser for an AIDS orphan project or another agency assisting AIDS-affected people.

Appendix 1

Gender-Based Proverbs

Traditional sayings and prayers are part of the fabric of our cultures. Although some of the proverbs below are no longer in common use, they still reflect deeply rooted attitudes toward women.

"A proper wife should be as obedient as a slave... The female is a female by virtue of a certain lack of qualities—a natural defectiveness."
—*Aristotle*

"A woman's place is at home or in the grave."
—*Pashtun Proverb, Afghanistan*

"A man loves first his son, then his camel, and then his wife."
"A woman's heaven is under the feet of her husband."
—*Arab Proverbs*

"Men are superior to women on account of the qualities with which God has gifted the one above the other, and on account of the outlay they make of their substance for them."
—*Quran, 4:34*

"If a wife dies, it is like a blow on the ankle. If a husband dies, it is like a blow on the head." —*Punjabi Proverb*

"The birth of a girl, grant elsewhere; here, grant a boy."
—*Ancient Atharva Veda of India*

"Lord, I thank thee that I was not born a woman."
—*Part of the morning prayer of the Orthodox Jew*

"When an ass climbs a ladder, we may find wisdom in a woman."

"A woman, a dog, and a walnut tree, the more you beat them the better they be."
—*Yoruba (Nigeria) Proverbs*

"A woman and an invalid man are the same thing."
—*Kikuyu (Kenya) Proverb*

"She is born a woman because she committed a thousand sins in the previous world." —*Buddhist Saying*

"Women are human but lower than men."

"It is the law of nature that women should not be allowed any will of her own."
—*Confucius, China*

"There are three unfilial acts: the greatest of these is the failure to produce sons." —*Mencius, a disciple of Confucianism*

"If you have a son, you can say you have a descendant. But you cannot say thus, even if you have ten daughters." —*Vietnam*

"Men are like gold; women are like white cloth." —*Cambodia*

"Women have long hair and a short mind." — *Sweden*

"There are no wise women." —*Japan*

"A man without brains and a woman without a man will never stand on their own legs." —*Estonia*

"A barn, a fence and a woman always need mending."
—*United States*

"To keep your wife on the rails, beat her—and if she goes off the rails, beat her." —*Puerto Rico and Spain*

"Beat your wife regularly... If you don't know why, she will."
—*Zambia*

"Affection begins at the end of a rod."—*Korea*

"Women, like dogs: the more you beat them, the more they love you." —*Argentina*

"The nails of a cart and the head of a woman: they work only when they are hit hard." —*Rajasthan, India*

"Love well, whip well." —*England*

Appendix 2
Useful Websites

Each of us can help turn the tide for girls and women caught in the tragedies described in this book. The internet sites listed below are only a representative selection of organizations and campaigns that can help you learn more, and that you might choose to support.

AIDS
The Global Coalition on Women and AIDS   http://www.womenandaids.net
World AIDS Day   http://www.worldaidsday.org/

Childbirth
Ethiopiaid   www.ethiopiaid.org.uk
Every Mother Counts   www.everymothercounts.org/
The Fistula Foundation   www.fistulafoundation.org/
Freedom from Fistula Foundation   www.freedomfromfistula.com
UN Population Fund   www.unfpa.org/public/mothers
Women Deliver   www.womendeliver.org/
Worldwide Fistula Fund   http://worldwidefistulafund.org

Child Labor
Anti-slavery Society   http://anti-slaverysociety.addr.com/slaverysasia.htm
Dalit Freedom Network (India)   http://www.dalitnetwork.org/
Do Something.org
   http://www.dosomething.org/tipsandtools/background-sweatshops
Child Labor Coalition   http://www.stopchildlabor.org/
Childs Rights and You (CRY—India)   www.cry.org
Fair Wear Campaign (Australia)   http://www.fairwear.org.au/
Free to Work, a project of "Not for Sale"   www.free2work.org
Global March Against Child Labour
   http://www.globalmarch.org/issues/Child-Labour
International Labour Organization   www.ilo.org
No Child Labour (Canada)   http://nochildlabour.org
The Young Center for Immigrant Children's Rights (USA)
   www.theyoungcenter.org/

Child Marriages
Girls Not Brides   http://girlsnotbrides.org/
Help the Child Brides (USA)   www.helpthechildbrides.com
Plan-UK Petition against early and forced marriages:
http://www.plan-uk.org/what-we-do/campaigns/because-i-am-a-girl/get-involved/take-the-vow/

Child Soldiers
Amnesty International http://web.amnesty.org/pages/childsoldiers-index-eng
Child Soldiers International   www.child-soldiers.org
Child Victims of War   childvictimsofwar.org.uk
Save the Children   http://www.savethechildren.org/
War Child International   www.warchild.org
Zero under 18 Campaign   http://www.zerounder18.org/

Deaf
Deaf Ministries International   www.deafmin.org/
Deaf Missions   www.deafmissions.com
Deaf Peoples   http://deafpeoples.imb.org/
Deaf World Ministries   www.deafworldministries.com/
D.O.O.R. International (Deaf Opportunity Out Reach
                                            www.doorinternational.com
Silent Blessings   www.silentblessings.org/
Story Runners   www.storyrunners.com/strategies/storyone-deaf-mission
World Federation for the Deaf   www.wfdeaf.org/

Disabled - General (See also "Violence to Disabled Women")
Ecumenical Disability Advocates Network   www.edan-wcc.org/
Joni and Friends   www.joniandfriends.org
Through the Roof   www.throughtheroof.org/

Domestic Violence
Iranian & Kurdish Women's Rights Organisation (UK)   http://ikwro.org.uk
Say No—Unite to End Violence   http://saynotoviolence.org/
Stop Violence Against Women http://www.stopvaw.org/Domestic_Violence2
Note: Be aware that local telephone books as well as internet searches can
provide 24-hour domestic violence helplines and services available in many
countries and cities.

Education
Children in Crisis   www.childrenincrisis.org/
Day of the Girl   http://dayofthegirl.org
Global Campaign for Education   http://campaignforeducation.org
Plan International   www.plan-uk.org/
Save the Children   www.savethechildren.org/
10X10 Campaign   http://10x10act.org/
UN Special Envoy for Global Education   educationenvoy.org
United Nations Girls Education Initiative   http://www.ungei.org/
World Vision   http://www.worldvision.org/our-work/education

Female Genital Mutilation (FGM)
Amnesty International   www.amnesty.org/

Desert Flower Foundation   www.desertflowerfoundation.org/en/
END FGM European Campaign   http://www.endfgm.eu/en/
Equality Now   http://www.equalitynow.org/
STOP-FGM-NOW.COM   www.stop-fgm-now.com/
Note: Facebook and Twitter groups also have pages dedicated to this issue, like
STOP FGM

Female Infanticide
The 50 Million Missing Campaign (India)
                          http://50millionmissing.wordpress.com/
Gendercide Watch   http://www.gendercide.org/
Society for the Protection of Unborn Children (China)   www.spuc.co.uk
Women's Rights Without Frontiers (China)
                          http://www.womensrightswithoutfrontiers.org/

Fistula - see Childbirth

Health Issues - General
Global Alliance for Women's Health   www.gawh.org/home.php5

Honor Killings
Facebook: International Campaign Against Honour Killings
Gendercide Watch   www.gendercide.org
Stop Honour Killings   www.stophonourkillings.com/

Muslim Women
Sawera (Pakistan)
http://www.asafeworldforwomen.org/partners-in-asia/partners-in-pakistan/sawera.html
Women Against Shariah   http://www.womenagainstshariah.com/
Women Living Under Muslim Laws   www.wluml.org/
Young Women for Change (Afghanistan)
                          http://www.youngwomenforchange.org/

Poverty
Dalit Freedom Network (India)   www.dalitnetwork.org/
Food for the Hungry   www.fh.org/
Food for the Poor   www.foodforthepoor.org/
Freedom from Hunger   www.freedomfromhunger.org]
Homeless International   www.homeless-international.org/
The Hunger Site   www.thehungersite.com
Urban Neighbours of Hope   http://www.unoh.org/

Rape as a Weapon of War - See "Women in War Zones"

Refugees

Refugee Highway Partnership	http://www.refugeehighway.net/
UN Refugee Agency	www.unhcr.org
Refugees International	www.refintl.org
Women's Refugee Commission	www.womenscommission.org/
Worldwide Refugee Information	www.refugees.org

Religious Slaves

Anti-Slavery International
    http://anti-slaverysociety.addr.com/slaverysasia.htm

EveryChild	http://www.everychild.org.uk/devadasi
Every Child Ministries (Africa)	http://www.ecmafrica.org/36223.ihtml
International Needs	http://www.ineeds.org.uk/
Servants of the Goddess	www.servantsofthegoddess.com
Sweetwater Ministries (Ghana)	sweetwaterhouse.org/

Street Kids

Action for Street Kids (ASK)	http://action4streetkids.org.uk/
Action International	www.actioninternational.org/
Child Hope	www.Childhope.org.uk
Every Child Ministries (Africa)	http://www.ecmafrica.org/
International Day for Street Children	www.streetchildrenday.org/
International Street Kids	www.internationalstreetkids.com
Railway Children (UK)	www.railwaychildren.org.uk
Street Kids for Christ (Philippines)	www.streetkids.net/
Teen Challenge	Globaltc.org
Toybox (Latin America)	www.toybox.org.uk
Viva Network for Children at Risk	http://www.viva.org
War Child	Warchild.org.uk

Traffic in Women & Girls

Coalition Against Trafficking in Women	www.catwinternational.org/

ECPAT (End Child Prostitution, Pornography & Trafficking of Children for Sexual Purposes) www.ecpat.net/

Free for Life International	www.freeforlifeintl.org/
Global Alliance Against Traffic in Women	www.gaatw.org/
Human Trafficking.org	www.humantrafficking.org/
Manna Freedom	www.mannafreedom.com
Not for Sale	www.notforsalecampaign.org/
Stop the Traffik	www.stopthetraffik.org/

Transnational Action Against Child Trafficking (TACT)
    http://tdh-childprotection.org

Violence to Disabled Women

Violence Against Women	www.vaw.umn.edu/

Widows
Appeal for Widows   http://appealforwidows.org/
Helping Orphans and Widows (H.O.W.)   http://acthow.org/
Afghan Renascent Youth Association (ARYA)   www.aryahelps.org/
Widows Care Worldwide   www.widowscareworldwide.org/
Widows' Rights International   www.widowsrights.org/

Women in War Zones
HEAL Africa   www.healafrica.org/empowering-women/
Synergy of Women for Victims of Sexual Violence
                              http://www.donordirectaction.org/synergie/
Women for Women International   www.womenforwomen.org
Women in War Zones   www.womeninwarzones.org/

Other Recommended Human Rights Sites About Women and Girls
A Safe World for Women   www.asafeworldforwomen.org
Girl Effect   www.girleffect.org
Human Rights Watch   www.hrw.org
Humanium   www.humanium.org
United Nations   www.un.org/womenwatch/,http://www.unwomen.org/
United Nations Development Fund for Women   www.unifem.org

Appendix 3

Suggested Books

Ali, Nujood, *I am Nujood, Age 10 and Divorced* (Crown, 2010).

Batstone, David, *Not For Sale: The Return of the Global Slave Trade* (Revised & Updated, HarperOne, 2010).

Belles, Nita, *In Our Backyard: A Christian Perspective on Human Trafficking in the United States* (Xulon, 2011).

Brooks, Geraldine, *Nine Parts of Desire: The Hidden World of Islamic Women* (London: Hamish Hamilton, 1995).

Chang, Leslie T., *Factory Girls: From Village to City in a Changing China* (Spiegel & Grau, 2008).

Dirie, Waris, *Desert Flower* (William Morrow, 1998).

Haugen, Gary, *Good News About Injustice: A Witness of Courage in a Hurting World* (InterVarsity Press, 2009, 1999).

Haugen, Gary, *Terrify No More* (Thomas Nelson, 2005).

Henry, Sharon, *Radhika's Story: Surviving Human Trafficking* (New Holland, 2010).

Hosseini, Khaled, *A Thousand Splendid Suns* (London: Bloomsbury, 2007).

Jewell, Dawn Herzog, *Escaping the Devil's Bedroom* (Kregel, 2008).

Kara, Siddarth, *Bonded Labor: Tackling the System of Slavery in South Asia* (Columbia University Press, 2012.

Kristof, Nicholas D. and Sheryl WuDunn, *Half the Sky: Turning Oppression Into Opportunity for Women Worldwide* (Knopf, 2009).

Lloyd, Rachel, *Girls Like Us: Fighting for a World Where Girls Are Not for Sale, an Activist Finds Her Calling and Heals Herself* (Harper Perennial, 2011).

Love, Fran and J. Eckheart, eds, *Ministry to Muslim Women: Longing to Call Them Sisters* (William Carey Library, 2000).

Muhsen, Zana and A. Crofts, *SOLD: One Woman's True Account of Modern Slavery* (Time Warner, 1994).

Nazer, Mende and Damien Lewis, *Slave: The True Story of a Girl's Lost Childhood and Her Fight for Survival* (Virago, 2007).

Parshall, Phil and Julie, *Lifting the Veil; The World of Muslim Women* (Georgia, US: Gabriel Publishing, 2002).

Roper, Matt, *Street Girls: Hope on the Streets of Brazil* (UK: Paternoster Lifestyle, 2001).

See, Lisa, *Snow Flower and the Secret Fan* (Random House, 2005).

Shakib, Siba, *Afghanistan, Where God Only Comes to Weep* (London: Century, 2002).

Shannon, Lisa, *A Thousand Sisters: My Journey into the Worst Place on Earth to Be a Woman* (Seal Press, 2010).

Shelley, Louise, *Human Trafficking: A Global Perspective* (Virginia, George Mason University, 2010).

Westwater, Julie, *Street Kid: One Child's Desperate Fight for Survival* (Harper Element, 2006).

Worden, Minky, *The Unfinished Revolution: Voices from the Global Fight for Women's Rights* (The Policy Press, 2012).

Appendix 4

7 Ways to Sharpen Your World Vision

1. Ask God to remove any "blind spots" you may have developed. Pray that he will open the eyes of your heart, so that you can see the world as He does.

2. Develop your awareness. Form a habit of jotting down world news items from the newspaper, radio or TV, and use them as a springboard for intercession.

3. Practice Acts 20:20 vision.--Go "house to house!" Develop the habit of prayer walking (or jogging) as you pass homes. Cultivate a friendship with a neighbor, perhaps one not born in your country. You may be surprised at how warmly you are received if you approach others as a learner, genuinely interested in understanding their culture.

4. Keep stretching your mind and heart. Reach into unknown horizons through articles, books, and TV documentaries. Use prayer guides like *Operation World.* Set a goal of remembering something new each time.

5. Take an active interest in the mission work your church supports. Get to know the missionaries by reading and praying over their updates. Invite them to your home if you get a chance.

6. Invest some of your hard-earned money in an overseas project.--A sure way to focus your interest!

7. Consider using a holiday to participate in a mission project this year, either at home or abroad. Mission agencies offer a wide range of fascinating opportunities throughout the year. You'll return home with much more than a tan!